# SCHOOLING, DIASPORA AND GENDER

*feminist educational thinking*

Series Editors:
**Kathleen Weiler**, Tufts University, USA
**Gaby Weiner**, Umeå University, Sweden
**Lyn Yates**, University of Technology, Australia

This authoritative series explores how theory/practice and the development of advanced ideas within feminism and education can be fused. The series aims to address the specific theoretical issues that confront feminist educators and to encourage both practitioner and academic debate.

Published and forthcoming titles:

# SCHOOLING, DIASPORA AND GENDER
Being feminist and being different

GEORGINA TSOLIDIS

**OPEN UNIVERSITY PRESS**
Buckingham · Philadelphia

Open University Press
Celtic Court
22 Ballmoor
Buckingham
MK18 1XW

email: enquiries@openup.co.uk
world wide web: www.openup.co.uk

and
325 Chestnut Street
Philadelphia, PA 19106, USA

First Published 2001

A catalogue record of this book is available from the British Library

ISBN    0 335 19630 6 (pb)    0 335 19631 4 (hb)

*Library of Congress Cataloging-in-Publication Data*
Tsolidis, Georgina.
    Schooling, diaspora, and gender : being feminist and being different / Georgina Tsolidis.
        p. cm. – (Feminist educational thinking)
    Includes bibliographical references and index.
    ISBN 0-335-19631-4 – ISBN 0-335-19630-6 (pbk.)
    1. Minority women–Education–Australia. 2. Women–Education–Australia. 3. Feminism and education – Australia. I. Title. II. Series.

LC2487.T86 2001
371.822′0994–dc21                                                              00-060639

Typeset by Type Study, Scarborough
Printed in Great Britain by St Edmundsbury Press, Bury St Edmunds, Suffolk

Dedicated to the memory of:

Phil Noyce and his belief that education could change the world

Solon Tsolidis and his belief that education could change the person

# Contents

# Series editors' preface

At the end of the twentieth century it is not a new idea to have a series on feminist educational thinking – feminist perspectives on educational theory, research, policy and practice have made a notable impact on these fields in the final decades of the century. But theory and practice have evolved, and educational and political contexts have changed. In contemporary educational policy debates, economic efficiency rather than social inequality is a key concern; what happens to boys is drawing more interest than what happens to girls; issues about cultural difference interrupt questions about gender; and new forms of theory challenge older frameworks of analysis. This series represents feminist educational thinking as it takes up these developments now.

Feminist educational thinking views the intersection of education and gender through a variety of lenses: it examines schools and universities as sites for the enacting of gender; it explores the ways in which conceptions of gender shape the provision of state-supported education; it highlights the resistances subordinated groups have developed around ideas of knowledge, power and learning; and it seeks to understand the relationship of education to gendered conceptions of citizenship, the family and the economy. Thus feminist educational thinking is fundamentally political; it fuses theory and practice in seeking to understand contemporary education with the aim of building a more just world for women and men. In so doing, it acknowledges the reality of multiple 'feminisms' and the intertwining of ethnicity, race and gender.

Feminist educational thinking is influenced both by developments in feminist theory more broadly and by the changing global educational landscape. In terms of theory, both post-structuralist and post-colonial theories have profoundly influenced what is conceived of as 'feminist'. As is true elsewhere, current feminist educational thinking takes as central the intersecting forces that shape the educational experiences of women and men. This emphasis on the construction and performances of gender through both discourses and material practices leads to an attitude of openness and questioning of accepted assumptions – including the underlying assumptions of the various strands of feminism.

In terms of the sites in which we work, feminist educational thinking increasingly addresses the impact of 'globalization' – the impact of neo-laissez-faire theories on education. As each of us knows all too well, the schools and universities in which we work have been profoundly affected by the growing dominance of ideas of social efficiency, market choice, and competition. In a rapidly changing world in which an ideology of profit has come to define all relationships, the question of gender is often lost, but in fact it is central to the way power is enacted in education as in society as a whole.

The books in this series thus seek to explore the ways in which theory and practice are interrelated. They introduce a third wave of feminist thinking in education, one that takes account of both global changes to the economy and politics, and changes in theorizing about that world. It is important to emphasize that feminist educational thinking not only shapes how we think about education but what we do *in* education – as teachers, academics, and citizens. Thus books within the series not only address the impact of global, national and local changes of education, but what specific space is available for feminists within education to mount a challenge to educational practices which encourage gendered and other forms of discriminatory practice.

*Kathleen Weiler*
*Gaby Weiner*
*Lyn Yates*

# Preface

I first came across Georgina Tsolidis in the early 1980s when feminist discussions of gender reforms were strong, and when there was beginning to be some explicit interest in difference among the broad category 'girls'. Most of the writing and policies at the time seemed to be busy building accounts of the double and triple disadvantages that made up the story of non-English-background girls and their schooling. Georgina Tsolidis was commissioned by a government body concerned with multiculturalism to undertake a study of these girls and she produced *Educating Voula*. This was not a study of the poor girls and their multiple oppressions. It was a story of strong and knowledgeable girls, girls with cultural and linguistic advantages, but girls who, nevertheless, were persistently isolated by their peers, underestimated by their teachers, and patronized by many serious feminist academics. This new story, an affirmative and challenging one, was a major intervention in the debates at that time.

Georgina Tsolidis is interested in, and identifies with, feminism, ethnicity and difference. Her focus is on education, and on how theory, practice and policy engage with her areas of concern. In this book, she moves both backwards and forwards from the foray I have described. Moving backwards (and outwards to other countries), Georgina Tsolidis sets the positioning of ethnic girls in Australian schools in the late twentieth century against a history of racism and changing constructions of the other. She shows how in Australia, at different times, different groups have been racialized: indigenous people, the Irish, southern Europeans, Vietnamese. For readers in other countries, the very unfamiliarity of some of the examples may seem to emphasize the point being made here that the categories of group identification, and of exclusion and racialization, are socially constructed ones.

Moving forwards, Georgina Tsolidis confronts an issue that is even more difficult. As she sometimes puts it, her own comfort zone was in identifying as an ethnic woman, and with a politics grounded in that body of experience and identification. Her challenge is where to go in the face of the subsequent feminist discussions that have so thoroughly problematized identity: gone was the comfort of speaking for and from the margins.

In this book, Georgina Tsolidis illustrates the changing location for research on ethnic minority girls and boys by a series of reflections on two different research projects she undertook, over a decade apart. Both used interviews with these students to attempt to understand the students' own understandings and positioning and the schooling processes that affected them. But the two projects were vastly different in the way the research was pursued. This book uses a discussion of the differences between a project of the early 1980s and a second project begun in the mid-1990s, and the author's concerns about her own positioning in the two projects, to shed light on theoretical, educational and research agendas concerning feminism and ethnic minority girls.

The case being made is that a feminist praxis of difference does need to take up issues of identification as well as issues of challenge or deconstruction. This in turn leads to the particular interest named in the title of this book, diasporic identity. Diasporic identities arise from in-between cultures, experiences of being both inside and outside the culture of the national setting. As such, Tsolidis argues, they are of great interest to contemporary debates about globalization and citizenship and what schooling might do in relation to these. Indeed, she argues, far from being a marginal concern to the main issues of schooling or gender reform, diasporic identifications can be a key pointer to transformative practices in schooling.

This book is grounded in the author's strong history of active engagement in the educational politics of these issues. It sets up a case which is not simply about what is done to minority groups in education, and not simply about how minority groups experience their education, but is an original contribution to feminist theorizing of difference, and schooling debates about students of minority cultural background.

*Lyn Yates*

# Acknowledgements

My mother Maria and my children Eirene and Alexis, without whose love, support and patience, this would not have been possible.

Lyn Yates, who suggested the project, helped it come to fruition and didn't lose her faith that it was in fact possible.

Eileen Sedunary for providing comments at short notice and at a time when the rest of us were weary.

Shona Mullen for her patience.

# I  Voicing difference

To find the perfect culture, I would like to select different parents and try another culture, and experience their living routine . . . If I marry a Greek or a Yugoslav, I expect that my husband would probably want me to follow his culture. Then I'd be divided into a thousand-piece jigsaw puzzle. When I had children, I'd expect to bring them up the good Australian way . . . I'm proud to be an Italian, but Australia is my home and I love it.

(MACMME, undated: 67)

Connie, an Italo-Australian in her last year of schooling, wrote this piece and entitled it, 'I'm like a jigsaw puzzle'. In her writing Connie reflected on being part of a minority community growing up in Australia. More than anything else, this book is about the positive nature of such cultural jigsaw puzzles. It is also an argument that young women, like Connie, play a pivotal role in putting this jigsaw puzzle together. In doing this they are bringing together different pieces to create a whole, distinct in nature from the pieces out of which it is made.

It is not uncommon for students like Connie to be considered through the framework of 'culture clash'. Unlike the violence, separation and conflict implicit in this common description, I interpret Connie's metaphor as one of bringing together, of making something out of multiples. Importantly, this is a process that requires evaluation and choice. She understands that the 'perfect culture' requires selection premised on lived experience and that this is tied up with birthright. Connie also engages with the emotional – the pride and love of both her heritage and homeland despite the fact that for her, these do not coincide. In her story, Connie contemplates the cultural birthright of her own children. She seems to understand the role of patriarchy in the family through her description of the expectation that women follow husbands. It is hoped, not too optimistically on my part, that there is a statement of resistance to this, in her comment that she would (instead?) bring them up 'the good Australian way'.

What is the 'good Australian way'? Implicit in this phrase exists a range of understandings related to culture. In Australia as elsewhere, the relationship between culture and nation is increasingly problematic. How is Connie's interpretation of the 'Australian way' created and changed by understandings of it which surround her? In turn, how are Connie's understandings changing those definitions, which already exist? In exploring these questions, I argue that schooling is a fundamental space in the creation of these diasporic identifications. It is at school that Connie will engage with the images and understandings of the 'Australian way' which are part of the public domain. She will also have the opportunity to evaluate the ways of her private domain, those of her family, in contradistinction to these. Similarly, she will contrast the private worlds of her Greek, Yugoslav and 'Australian' peers to the public face of the 'Australian way'. These complex interactions contribute to the contestation and reinscription of our public and private cultures.

Fundamentally, this is a book about diasporic identifications and the role of gender and schooling in their creation. This is also a feminist book. My argument is that because of the pivotal role of gender in the creation of diasporic identifications, it is quite sensible to expect that feminist theorizations of identity and difference will have something profound to say to educationists interested in the role of schooling in the creation of these identifications. Most particularly, I am drawn to feminist work concerned with the relationship between equity and difference. Not only does this work relate to diasporic identifications directly, but also it speaks to the often contemplated dilemma in education: that of offering students access to common and therefore socially empowering knowledges, in ways that do not assume that marginal groups of students need to unlearn their own cultures in order to succeed.

My overall intention is to argue that it is possible and valuable to be both feminist and different. I argue that within the politics of education, it is often the case that the acknowledged feminist voice is unitary and that this means different feminist voices are silenced. I argue that one of the results of this silencing is that students like Connie do not have the benefit of school-based feminist politics of difference and that as a result, diasporic identifications have more limited possibilities.

Given that no story, no knowledge, are neutral, I aim to situate my arguments, descriptions and research within my own social, cultural and political frames. This introduction has had many drafts. Re-reading a friend's comments on one of these, I realized that I had not resolved the issue of which voice I wanted to project into the public arena in a book bearing my name. She asked: Why the impersonal third person? Why the dry language of a government report? In this context, I was drawn, once again, to the concept of voice and the familiar feminist dilemmas and debates with which it is surrounded. What is it that I want to say and how is this entangled with the ways in which I want to say it, who I am and the ways in which it could be understood?

In thinking about these questions I was drawn to the comments of Magda Lewis (1993), in a chapter from her book *Without a Word*, which I use with my students in a postgraduate subject related to feminism and education. In the chapter entitled 'Beginnings', Lewis makes the statement:

> From my own experience, I know that not all of what appears to women's silence is the absence of discourse. Infused with the context of my own lived realities, the text of this book gives integrity and political meaning to my own silences, grown, as I know they are, not out of inadequacy and deficiency, but of a deeply felt rage at those who live their unexamined privilege as entitlement.
>
> (Lewis 1993: 3)

In fundamental ways, this is a story about speaking; why the urge to speak, on what basis to speak, how to speak and in what language. It is situated in relation to my 'rage at those who live their unexamined privilege as entitlement'. It reflects a personal exploration of identifying privilege, the basis of its entitlement and why it can remain unexamined. At a general level I am interested in the potential of education to identify, examine and challenge privilege as entitlement. More specifically, I am interested in the role that feminism can play in this.

My own lived realities which infuse this interest and bring 'political meaning to my own silences' arise out of the contradictions of being an ethnic minority woman in Australia – the contradictions between the lived experience of this status as other than inadequacy and deficiency, and the representations of this status as inadequacy and deficiency. To some extent it is a product of a rage triggered by what I identify as a reluctance within some aspects of mainstream feminism to come to terms with its own privilege. This is a privilege I initially understood in the early 1980s as not having to choose between enemies: for 'them' it was just a matter of sexism, while for 'us' it was a matter of racism *or* sexism. Since then I have turned to the work of antiracist feminists in an attempt to understand both this type of feminist privilege and this type of feminist rage. I have turned my mind to the constitution of identity; identity as it is attributed by others in derogatory terms and the corollary of this, the strident constitution of it in reactive and defensive ways. I have also turned to the role of schooling in relation to these issues.

At the heart of these explorations is an engagement with how we as feminists maintain our willingness and capacity to enact change in ways that do not assume a unitary voice. How do we challenge unitary understandings of what it is we wish to change? How do we understand the limitations of a unitary vision of how change is constituted and the means by which it can be enacted? In other words, how do we remain both feminist *and* different?

The context for this exploration is education – by and large, secondary schooling in Australia. This context represents my professional experience. In doing so, it is also a reflection of my belief in the significance of education as a potential means of changing both society and the lives of individuals. This view of education has a long history in Australia, as elsewhere and in terms of my own life it has been most influential.

A child of immigrant parents, I began school with no English and was the only one in my extended family to enter university. I began university the year that Saigon fell, which was also the year that the Tertiary Education Assistance Scheme was introduced. This made it possible for Australian tertiary students to claim government financial support without this being pegged to a contract that bound them to pay this money back in real terms or in terms of employment, most commonly through teaching. This scheme reflected the emphasis that the then new Labor government was giving education. As a result, I am one of too few Australians who started school and finished university with a PhD and who did not have to pay a cent in fees for any part of this journey. In many ways my experience forms a snapshot of an era when there was great optimism surrounding the capacity of education to contribute to a form of social egalitarianism and it is not surprising that I carry this optimism with me still.

My concern with the limitations of a unitary feminist voice within the politics of educational change is grounded in my experience of life in Australia as a member of an ethnic minority community. The construction of ethnicity has great significance in Australia. Cultural difference and notions of (non) belonging are inscribed through ethnicity in ways that have limited parallels in countries where constructions of race overwhelm such difference. With its history of migration, the White Australia Policy and the more recent policy of multiculturalism, ethnicity has received much attention in Australia. This Australian experience of ethnicity has increasing relevance and application globally.

Evolving cultural understandings, which reflect and engage with the new economic and technological realities, throw into stark relief the interdependent, sometimes contradictory and dialectical relationships between the global and local. This relationship between specificity and universalism is exemplified in the lived experiences of groups such as Australian ethnic minorities. Members of such groups negotiate, on a daily basis, the relationship between difference and sameness – what makes them different within Australian society, as well as the societies of the countries they or their forebears left behind. Similarly, they negotiate what makes them the same as others, both in Australia and their countries of origin. Schooling is a particularly significant site for these considerations. The school is a space in which the public and the private are mediated. For many minority students it is where they first come to understand the familiar as different and recognize its construction as potentially problematic.

Various feminist debates offer a framework for exploring such considerations. First, within feminism there has been sustained debate around the relationship between identity and difference. Second, the role of gender is critical to the establishment of community as it pertains both to ethnic collectivities and to public pedagogies related to citizenship: as a consequence, the feminist theorization of related issues is most insightful.

Throughout my schooling, I was confronted by the label 'Greek'. This meant various things. For some teachers it meant that I could not achieve despite the fact that I was achieving, even in their classes. One of my most vivid memories is of my economics teacher in my last year of schooling telling my father I had little chance of passing the final examinations because of English language difficulties. At the time I was receiving grade As for English and above average passes in economics. I also remember my father accusing this teacher of racism during a very heated exchange. On the other hand, for the Hellenophile art teacher, being Greek meant that I had some historic and presumably genetic link with the art world of Ancient Greece. As a result, he had to reconcile this belief and his regular disappointment with the fact that my art prowess did not measure up to his imagination of its potential.

At home, being Greek was linked to being different from the others: pride in a heritage linked to a distant homeland, linguistic and cultural maintenance, the prioritization of academic achievement, and a social life which was family and community based, cosmopolitan and sophisticated. I grew up surrounded by individuals each of whom spoke four or five languages, people who were well travelled. While the notions of cosmopolitanism and diaspora have taken on significantly new theoretical meanings, in their lived form they have been commonplace in my family and the families of those like me. My grandparents, individually and at various times and for various reasons left Cyprus and two small islands in the Dodecanese respectively. They grew up, married and had children in different cities in Egypt. I was the first of a generation within my extended family not born and educated in Egypt. My family came to Australia via what is now Botswana and Zimbabwe, where I was born. Throughout my life I have been accustomed to forms of cosmopolitanism, to understandings that I have family in the USA, the UK, in Africa, in Australia, as well as in Greece and Cyprus. My mother writes to school friends who now live in Belgium and Johannesburg and she does so in Greek. When we visit Greece and Cyprus, many of the family we meet, at the houses of relatives we have in common, are also 'tourists'. Together we add to the burden of the cluttered mantelpieces of those who stayed behind, mantelpieces which strain under photographs of relatives never met as well as souvenirs: the small kangaroos, wooden African carvings and placemats from Sydney or Bulawayo or London, all telling the stories of these multiple migrations.

We arrived in Australia when I was 10 years old. In the 1960s, Australian society was struggling to come to grips with the fact that it was not just the British who were migrating to its shores. Australian government policy was attempting to find ways of making the non-British appear British in the public imagination. This was a step in the demographic transition which would result in Australia becoming one of the most culturally and linguistically diverse nations in the world. It is so often women who are seen as the embodiment of such processes through their sexuality, their role as mothers and the expectation that through this role, they are both caretakers and conduits for the transfer of the common culture. Not surprisingly for me at school, the term 'Greek' was linked to certain notions of 'girl' and a range of understandings about what it meant to be a Greek girl. Greek girls were not allowed out. Greek girls were not able to attend school camps. Greek girls were not allowed to have boyfriends. Greek girls had to be 'good girls' and consequently Greek girls strained at the leash of their policed sexuality, given that they were also 'buxom', 'earthy' and 'mature' (rather than a description of a state of mind, 'mature' was often used by teachers to denote reaching puberty relatively early).

In Australia ethnicity remains a significant way of understanding relationships between minorities and majorities; between perpetually transient Australians, the so-called second- and third-generation migrants from countries such as Greece and Italy and the 'real' Australians. This perpetual transience is captured by comments such as, 'Why don't you go back home?' and 'Go back to where you came from'. In 1997 after over thirty years' residency in Australia, my perpetual transience was brought home to me when once again, I was told to go back to where I came from. I was at a forum on Australian multiculturalism and new forms of racism where a colleague, who identifies as black and who has a familial link to India, was speaking. Members of the audience who were keen opponents of immigration began to harangue some speakers and their supporters. It was in this context that I was told to go back to Calcutta, accused of taking the jobs of Australians, and jostled.

Clearly the lived experience of racism is complex. I struggle to articulate this particular example without, on the one hand, wishing to detract from the real differences between myself and those from minorities which are most often racialized, and on the other hand, reinforcing such dichotomies by naming them as more or less significant. In this instance, had I denied being from Calcutta I would have confirmed 'the problem' with Calcutta; yet accepting my link to Calcutta would have denied the differences between experiences of racism. Whiteness and blackness are not immutable categories and as social and political constructs they remain complex and problematic. When I began school without any English in what was then Rhodesia, I looked extremely different from my generally blonde and blue-eyed peers and my experiences of racism were profound. Yet I lived in Africa, and because of the racism which existed in Rhodesia, I did not share my classroom or my neighbourhood with Black Africans. In this way, my experience of racism was also an exemplar of my 'European' privilege.

The relationship between racism, belonging and embodiment is complex. Hage (1998) refers to 'Third World-looking migrants' in his attempt to disentangle the various forms of non-belonging in Australia. He argues that whiteness 'is an aspiration that one accumulates various capitals to try to be' (Hage 1998: 60). He points to the paradox that

> no matter how much capital one acquires through active accumulation, the very fact of this acquired capital being an *accumulation* leads to its devaluing relative to those who posit themselves to have inherited it or to possess it innately without having to accumulate it.
>
> (Hage 1998: 64, original emphasis)

It remains significant that in Australia, being part of an ethnic minority makes one vulnerable at least, to accusations of non-belonging. This vulnerability is somehow linked to understandings of Australianness which have British cultural underpinnings and an imagined embodiment – the bronzed, blonde and blue-eyed. Whether one falls short of this imagined embodiment due to Mediterranean or Indian ancestry, for example, is clearly irrelevant for those for whom 'we' all look the same.

My first teaching appointment was at a secondary school where approximately 60 per cent of the students had a Greek background and an additional 20 per cent were variously from Italian, Lebanese and Turkish backgrounds. These were students whose parents had migrated so that their children would have more opportunities. These parents worked in factories, their children had to acquire English in order to succeed and in some cases they would enter university as a result of much hard work and some good luck.

Since then the constitution of Australian ethnicity in the public imagination has become more rather than less complex. It is increasingly difficult to make ethnicity synonymous with migrancy because students such as those I have described have married and had children of their own, more and more often in relationships that cross cultural and linguistic boundaries. Added to this is the increasing movement between countries so that migrations are multiple and do not necessarily assume ongoing settlement in the country of destination. Also altered are the source countries and motivations for migration. No longer can we assume that the immigrants will be the poor and wartorn in search of a better life.

Despite such changes, the questions that arose out of my first teaching experience remain those that still fascinate me. At the foundation of these questions is the construction of cultural difference as problematic rather than positive. The role of schooling in the assimilationist agenda, for example, would not be an issue if difference were seen as positive. Similarly, the potential for feminism to support such an assimilationist agenda would not be a possibility.

The construction of cultural difference as problematic prompts the same concerns whether the students are Greek, Vietnamese or Chinese. Moreover, such an understanding of difference does not exist only in the minds of teachers like my economics teacher, who became a teacher after leaving the armed forces and who fitted the stereotype associated with this background at the time – conservative, nationalistic and culturally narrow.

My initial teaching experience coincided with a time of great change within education in the State of Victoria. Through a range of networks including teacher unions and parent organizations, what was being taught and how this was taught and assessed were being challenged and reconstituted. The move was towards school-based and student-centred curriculum, pedagogy and assessment. As part of this, teacher professionalism was also changing. Rather than curriculum being determined centrally and delivered by teachers whose students would be assessed through externally set examinations, teachers were demanding the right to develop their own curriculum and methods of assessment. At the heart of this burgeoning radicalism was the fundamental issue of the means by which some knowledge over and above other knowledge is constituted as socially significant through its selection for teaching and learning. Not surprisingly these politics related to socially valuable knowledge were accelerated by marginal groups attempting to make 'their knowledges' socially significant through schooling. Languages such as Greek, Italian, Arabic and Turkish replaced French and German in many schools. There was also a feminist incursion that placed women's studies and women's ways of knowing on the agenda at many schools.

It was through this experience at the school level that I initially encountered the very real problems of political movement premised on essentialist understandings. For many of the feminist teachers involved in this grassroots movement, which arguably led to a range of State and national policy initiatives in the area, being feminist and being different to their vision of feminist was not possible. This relationship between mainstream feminism and cultural difference has a long history and is explored in detail in subsequent chapters.

The fact that this book is an engagement with feminism reflects my priorities: it is the movement from which I expected the most and it is the movement with which I still identify. It is also the movement about which I remain most optimistic. This statement belies a range of theoretical positionings that I shall delve into further in subsequent chapters. At this stage, suffice it to state that I am still convinced of the merits of the feminist movement, hence my concern with how it can be achieved in ways that take account of difference. I am still optimistic about the possibility that within feminism, we can engage with new forms of praxis which are responsive to what Stuart Hall describes as the 'new times' (Hall 1996b).

The argument made by Hall that we live in 'new times', a component of which are 'new ethnicities', diasporic in character, is one which frames the arguments made here. It is increasingly impossible to understand ethnicity as static and linked to a specific place or people. The relevance of the nation-state and the possibility of cultural specificity in light of global movement and technological developments have come under considerable scrutiny. Bauman (1997) recognizes as a key feature of our postmodern era the liability of a fixed identity. Instead of striving to discover, invent or construct an identity, he argues that

> Well-sewn durable identity is no more an asset; increasingly and ever-more evidently, it becomes a liability. *The hub of postmodern life strategy is not making identity stand – but the avoidance of being fixed.*
> (Bauman, 1997: 89, original emphasis)

Yet our everyday realities in schools and elsewhere indicate that the 'new times', like the old ones, are full of unequal power relations which are lived and embodied in various ways. Indeed, the postmodern dynamic away from fixed identity may at particular moments create a dynamic in the opposite direction. The relationship between the global and the local or the universal and the specific have forced us to consider unequal power relations anew. Is it possible to and if so, how is it possible to constitute diasporic identities in ways that challenge rather than reinscribe hegemonic power relations?

Schooling, particularly during adolescence, is an important context for processes of identification. For minority students in particular, these are times when the public and private worlds meet in the school yard and in the classroom and understandings develop related to the various estimations of both. Rather than pursue this theme through the common model of culture clash, here schooling will be explored as a site where the private and public have the potential to form a dialectical relationship that can produce new identifications representative of new cultural formations. Most specifically, the intention is to explore the role of gender in the development of these new cultural formations. Because of this intention, feminist theorizations of identity and difference are pivotal to the argument.

While the debate about equality and difference within feminism has traditionally been established *vis-à-vis* men, increasingly it is framing explorations of the category 'women' and within it, the differences which exist. In this context, 'ethnicity' takes on a parallel meaning to difference, and gender does so for equality. Additionally, notions of cultural difference are imperative for understanding and educating for the 'new times'. Following from this, two further arguments are made in this book: that gender is critical for the understanding of cultural difference and that explorations of Australian ethnicity have much to offer debates about cultural difference and schooling in the context of the 'new times' more generally. It is in this sense that the book is framed in relation to diasporic identifications.

The relationship between equity and difference is critical. It has preoccupied many concerned with education, and in different ways has been a cornerstone of various feminist debates. Within the field of education the debate has different sets of meanings. One of the contentions in this book is that the debates within feminism related to difference and equality, particularly as it applies within the category 'women', provides valuable insights for the educational debate. A particular aim is to use feminist theorizations of equity and difference to shed light on the way we understand educational equity and how we understand difference in relation to it. Can a feminist politics of difference assist us as educators to break down the traditionally inscribed binary between equity and difference? In terms that close the circle on the biographical notes which opened this introduction: were my educational needs met because my life history coincided with a period when a reformist Labor government positioned tertiary education as potentially socially transformative and made it free? Can we peg the potential of education to change social inequality to a broad egalitarianism which changes the composition of that sector of society who have access to education or do we provide a range of different educations? Clearly this is not a new debate; however, I believe that feminist theorizations of equality and difference can help us to frame it anew.

In summary, the main arguments in this book are that schooling, particularly secondary schooling, is a significant site for processes of identification. Critical to the 'new times' are diasporic identifications and that the role of schooling in relation to these requires sustained consideration. Further to this, I argue that gender is most significant in the establishment of diasporic identifications. In this way, feminist theorizations of identity and difference, most particularly with reference to the equality and difference debate, have the potential to help us frame our understanding of the same debate as it relates to schooling in globalized times. These arguments are explored through research undertaken in Australian secondary schools over a ten-year period and through an exploration of related policy literature.

I have stated that one of my arguments relates to the positive nature of difference. The very fact that this can be constructed as an argument rather than simply being a truism, belies the fact that this is also a book about racism.

In Chapter 3, the argument is made that within Australia, mainstream feminist discourses concerned with education promulgated an essentialist understanding of 'girls'. This position is developed through a review of Australian gender equity education policies. Similarly, the argument is made that policies concerned with difference failed to highlight the specificity of female experience and that as a result, the articulation of gender and ethnicity remained invisible in both policy discourses. However, the intention is to go further than the illustration of such shortcomings. Within these policies we also see new directions which (I argue) indicate the possibility of challenging the established binary of equity and difference.

This essentialism is contextualized in Chapter 2. The construction of ethnicity in Australia is elaborated and in particular the role of gender within this is considered. Roles and representations of ethnic minority women in Australian society more generally are also explored.

In Chapters 4 and 5 I describe the processes whereby gender and ethnicity articulate in school-based constructions of diasporic identifications. In Chapter 4 I outline the Educating Voula study that was begun in 1984. Through it, I pay particular attention to student aspirations, socializing and sexuality within and across ethnic and gender categories. In Chapter 5 I describe the Bureau Study that was begun in 1994 and explore how minority students construct 'good' schooling and 'good' students in relation to diasporic identifications.

A feminist praxis which centres difference is explored in Chapter 6. The possibility of being feminist and remaining different presumes a feminist politics of difference. It is in this chapter that I explore the debates within feminism which (I subsequently argue in Chapter 7) are relevant to challenging the equality and difference binary within education.

In Australia with its history of migration, there has been an ongoing engagement with the 'new ethnicities' which are part of the 'new times'. While the relationship between the local and the global will have its own character bounded by the specificity of context, none the less, there exists potential for the relevance of this engagement beyond its own context. The Vietnamese, Chinese and Russian students, the Indian, Serbian and Greek students have left the same homelands for the same reasons. They experience similar contradictions related to who they are and representations of this, whether they live in the UK, USA, Canada or Australia. In globalized times academic work, like all else, will tell a story, the beginning of which may have started in one country, the middle of which is played out in another and the destination of its conclusion is yet to be determined. These beginnings, middles and conclusions are not separate case studies, they are the same story. In this sense, our work as academics is increasingly communal – more and more we are reliant on each other in order to bring meaning to our work.

# 2 Ethnicity as constructed difference: being an 'ethnic woman' in Australia

Bill had good cause to remember Toula. He had once heard his mother speak of her as a possible mate for himself before he had left for England ten years ago. . . . Bill found it difficult to resist looking at Toula. She looked so Greek to him: in his imagination those long loose curls of thick black hair that danced up and down every time she moved made her look as if she had just stepped off a Grecian vase. She was nothing like his red-haired wife in appearance, and Bill was suddenly struck by the fancy that, had he wanted it, he could have enjoyed a very different life.

(Athanasou 1995: 333–4)

Bill is a 'Grozzer', a Greek-Australian, and in this short passage, Athanasou captures the contradictions of diasporic identifications and their relationship to place, time and embodiment. Most particularly, he captures the articulation of gender and ethnicity and the pivotal role of sexuality and marriage within these identifications.

Historically, notions of 'race' and ethnicity have provided an obvious means of understanding the embodiment of power relations. At one level there is something innocuous about ethnicity, denoting as it does language, cultural traditions, a value system and perhaps a religion; yet at another level, the term has become entwined in the stuff of harder, more political narratives related to exclusion. We need to understand this shift in relation to the demise of 'race'. If we can no longer link racism to 'race', then somehow the innocence of ethnicity comes into question.

Many social theorists (Brittan and Maynard 1984; White 1985; Castles *et al.* 1988; de Lepervanche 1988; Miles 1988; Klug 1989; Ramazanoglu 1989; Anthias and Yuval-Davis 1992; Pettman 1992; Vasta and Castles 1996) argue that a range of ethnicities exist and that some of these, depending on time and place, will suffer racialization, that is, a particularly virulent form of marginalization, often invoking physical appearance to reinforce it. This position may have a particular currency among those who do not wish to reinscribe 'race' with meaning based on biology, but commonsense under-standings and usages create racist discourses which differentiate on the basis of appearance none the less. However, which appearances are targeted for racialization become time and place specific and far from straightforward. It is in the Australian context that the naming of ethnicity as a category of non-belonging takes on a particular significance that it seems not to have in other places. It has been argued that in the lexicon of 'othering', 'race' gave way to 'ethnicity' as a means of coming to terms with the demographic shifts which occurred in Australia due to post-Second World War immigration (de Lepervanche 1980). After the horrors of extermination camps and the implication within these horrors of the typologies made popular in pre-war social Darwinism, ethnicity was a softer, more acceptable way of denoting a particular type of difference linked to natural incompatibility and non-belonging.

Commonly, ethnicity is associated with language, customs, beliefs, religion or generally those characteristics which create and reproduce a cultural identity. Yuval-Davis and Anthias (1989) have argued that it is difficult to delineate between 'race', ethnicity and nationality because migration, colonization and conquest have developed such a heterogeneous body of historical cases. Instead they argue that ethnicity is an ideological construct used to divide people into collectivities, a process which, although primarily ideological, none the less involves real material practices. They argue that boundaries which exclude and include are constructed variously on the basis of tribe, nation, linguistic or cultural background and have in common the understanding that the individual is born into or placed naturally into such collectivities. Additionally they make the point that a national group makes a claim for separate political and territorial representation and that in English, the word 'nationality' tends to be synonymous with citizenship and in this way defines one's relationship with a particular state.

The significance of such a definition is its assumption that ethnicity belongs to everyone, not just minorities and cannot be separated from the socio-political construction of 'race'. There are clear examples of the racialization of various ethnicities responding to economic or political circumstances. For example, there have been periods in British history that have seen both Irish and Jewish people racialized. At times when particular ethnic groups have been racialized a biological veneer has been used to distinguish them from the mainstream. The stereotype alleged of the Jewish nose or the lower intellect of the Irish are examples of this. However, at this point in time in Britain, it is immigrant groups from its former colonies which are deemed problematic and the consequential racialization has given skin colour paramount significance. Racialization is responsive to changes in the economic or political factors which create it. This is evidenced by the South African example of the non-racialization of the Japanese, a development arguably related to their global economic ascendancy (Jakubowicz 1981;

Lawrence 1982a; Barrett and McIntosh 1985; de Lepervanche 1989; Klug 1989).

In Australia, the concept of ethnicity has been used to exclude Australian ethnic minorities from 'legitimate Australianness' and often, the economic and social power associated with it. While ethnic majority Australians, ethnic minority Australians and indigenous Australians are distinguished by a wide range of languages and 'countries', all have an ethnicity, but it is only the members of Australia's ethnic minorities who are generally conceived of as 'ethnics'. Terms such as 'new Australians', 'migrants' or 'ethnics' have been used to differentiate between 'real' and 'non-real' Australians, a fact with some irony when considered in relation to Australia's indigenous peoples (as will be discussed later in this chapter). There is a common conception that those with British ancestry are the 'real' Australians, playing host to lucky guests whose non-belonging is captured by the transience embedded in terms like 'migrant', often used to describe Australians who were either born in or spent most of their lives in Australia but whose parents were post-war immigrants. The same sentiments are conveyed in the self-contradictory terms 'second- and third-generation migrant'.

'Realness' in this context relates to power, which in Australia is linked to the establishment of a British colony and the subsequent British cultural hegemony. White (1985) makes the point, that as late as 1953, elements within Australian society were still referring to Australia as a British community and England as 'home'. While elements of this attitude persist to this day and are evidenced by the debates surrounding republicanism, for example, it is also clear that subsequent to the Second World War there has been an accelerated development of an Australian character or identity which is not tied to 'Britishness'. However, in itself, this has been linked to urbanization and the closer economic and cultural ties with the USA which occurred after the war (White 1985). In this context 'Australianness' is still being determined in relation to the ethnic majority and the direction of its identification rather than in relation to ethnic minorities and the impact they are having on the actual demographic and cultural make-up of Australian society.

A significant difficulty with a characterization which conflates ethnic majority and the common Australian usage of British is the fact that the term 'British' fails to distinguish the various ethnicities which are constituted within it. Most significantly, it fails to recognize the division between the Irish and the English which has been important, traditionally, in shaping the character of Australia. Within Australian society, the Irish are traditionally identified as the underdogs relative to the English. For example, there are Irish who came to Australia as convicts because of uprisings against the English in their homeland, they are identified with bushranging through figures like Ned Kelly, associated with the miners' rebellion at Eureka, identified with working-class traditions and perhaps most significantly, Catholicism

(McConville 1987). Although Irish Gaelic and Irish culture have a less distinct profile within modern-day Australia than many non-British languages and cultures, the force of resistance to the establishment by this community has lingered on in the form of such institutions as the Catholic education system (Jakubowicz 1981). The term Anglo-Celtic has been adopted by some in an effort to distinguish between the English and non-English elements subsumed within the term British (Yuval-Davis 1986; Foster 1988). However, this term too has been characterized as an offensive amalgam which glosses over very real historical, cultural and power differences (Castles *et al.* 1988).

Despite the power disparities and the different languages and cultures subsumed by the term 'British', it is these ethnicities that are constituted in political and social terms as the 'natural' Australians. While the Irish may in fact be underdogs to the English, there is still a clear distinction between the Irish, English, Welsh and Scottish traditions in Australian society, and those of other ethnicities; the former are constituted as Australian, be they Australian establishment or Australian anti-establishment, and the latter as foreign. The hegemonic definition of Australian, while extending to Irish Catholic, Scot or Welsh, does not extend to Greek, Italian, Arab or Vietnamese, regardless of length of residency. This is illustrated by the fact that terms such as 'new Australian', 'ethnic', 'migrant' or 'second-generation migrant' are applied to the latter groups but not the former.

The term 'ethnic minority' also subsumes a vast range of cultural, linguistic, class, age and gender diversity, as well as motive for, and experience of, migration. Often political, religious or geographic factors which are paramount in shaping an identity are lost under labels such as Chinese or Arabic, let alone a generic term like 'ethnic minority'. Such a term also glosses over the power differences that exist between men and women, old and new 'migrants', the moneyed and unmoneyed, the urban and rural, the economic and political refugees, the racialized and the unracialized.

## Ethnicity and racialization

In Australia, racialization is linked significantly to British colonialism and its impact on the indigenous peoples, underpinned as it was by social-Darwinist understandings of 'race' which created a hierarchy of peoples and cultures based on an assumption of British superiority. The late-nineteenth-century scientific obsession with classification extended to the exploration of national types. There was a belief that factors such as national prosperity and morality were a product of a national character and this notion was used to support the belief that the 'Anglo-Saxon race' was superior. There was great interest in whether this superiority would degenerate or progress in the colonies. The Australian national type was understood as the best of British stock combined with an environment which allowed outdoor living and sport. The understanding was that the British type would thrive, particularly in Australia, because unlike other colonies, 98 per cent of the population was British. However, this racial purity needed to be protected, especially in relation to the Aborigines and the Chinese (London 1970; de Lepervanche 1980; White 1985; McQueen 1986; Castles *et al.* 1988). Although racial categories have been applied to Indians, Kanakas and some European groups at various points in Australian history (London 1970; de Lepervanche 1980; York 1990), racialization has been most vehement in relation to the Aboriginal peoples and those deemed 'Asian'.

In Australia, the terms 'minority' and 'majority' most commonly stand outside black–white relations and are used to differentiate between the ethnic majority, seen as the 'real' Australians, and the 'new Australians'. This notion of 'Australianness' must be explored in the context of Aboriginal history. White occupation in Australia is just over 200 years old. In comparison, Aboriginal civilizations are at least 30,000 and possibly 100,000 years old. The distinction between 'real' and 'non-real' non-Aboriginal Australians needs to be considered in this context. The claim to legitimize 'Australianness' by those with British ancestry must be related to the colonization of Aboriginal Australia. Colonization established the British cultural hegemony which still characterizes mainstream Australian society, an important element of which is racism.

To provide a history of Aboriginal Australia which is not superficial is beyond the scope of this exercise; however, some comment is warranted. The Aboriginal history of Australia is important, not only because of the factual and moral imperative to refer to it, but also because it establishes that, relative to the Aborigines, all others are 'new Australians' and that claims to 'legitimate Australianness' by those with British ancestry are much more related to power than numerical majorities, time-frames or notions of pioneering. The concept of 'race' has been used to externalize the indigenous peoples of Australia and make them outsiders in their own country. This racism has framed Australian nationhood and began with the occupation of the land deemed *terra nullius* or uninhabited. This situation has been long-standing and has come into serious question only with the High Court Mabo ruling in 1992, which opened the door for native title claims (Reynolds 1996).

The social Darwinism of the British colonial period, in which the white occupation of Australia took place, understood the Aborigines to be nothing more than savages, barely above animals. Such an evolutionary perspective provided the justification for why the 'superior race', the British, would survive over a so-called primitive people like the Aborigines. Hughes (1988) quotes a settler who in 1849 commented that 'Nothing can stay the dying away of the Aboriginal race, which Providence has only allowed to hold the land until replaced by a finer race' (Hughes 1988: 7). This view has lingered and it was not until 1967 that Aborigines were granted the status of citizens after a referendum which gave the Commonwealth the authority to act on their behalf (Macintyre 1985).

The legacy of this racism is twofold. On the one hand, indigenous peoples have been traditionally denied their history. Attwood (1996) argues that history is the study of the past in an ongoing relationship with the present and future. Because the Aboriginal peoples of Australia were considered to have no future, they became the domain of anthropologists, considered artefacts of a doomed civilization. On the other hand, aspects of their cultures, such as spiritual links to the land and thousands of years of occupation, in other contexts, have been romanticized by whites. As a result, they have been entrusted with the burden of authenticity: of creating for Australia a distinctive national identity. Globalization is characterized by a profound tension between homogeneity and difference. As the world becomes more accessible and familiarity increases, there is a search for 'exotic' worth. In this context, being different from that which is accessible is increasingly elusive and therefore increasingly valuable. In this way, this type of authenticity has a particular currency.

The racialization of non-Aboriginal groups has related strongly to Australian immigration policy. There has been an historic fear that due to Australia's geographic location, Asian immigration would threaten the existing British hegemony. Legislation in the form of the White Australia Policy and, before it, legislation enacted in Victoria and New South Wales to keep out Chinese gold-diggers, has had the principal aim of keeping out the 'yellow peril'. The perceived threat posed by Asian immigration has had an economic element, particularly obvious during the Gold Rushes; however, 'Economic fears and racial prejudice were by now inextricable, with each feeding the flames of the other's fire' (McQueen 1986: 33).

Immigration debates tend to focus on inclusion and exclusion and assume that the desired end-point is successful integration into the existing population which is understood in hegemonic terms. Appearance and cultural practices are used to highlight the non-belonging of the groups to be excluded. During the Gold Rushes, Chinese appearance was used to deride and instance the alleged inferiority of Chinese people. Similarly, the use of opium and allegations of lustfulness and the threat that this posed to local women were given as reasons why they needed to be excluded. In addition, particular work practices, such as docility, have been associated with the Chinese and these judged a threat to existing Australian labour practices, particularly by the union movement (de Lepervanche 1980; McQueen 1986).

Such attitudes to Asian immigration are still evident in more recent immigration debates. Although Australian government departments have often included Turkey and the Middle East in definitions of Asia (Department of Immigration and Ethnic Affairs 1986) commonsense understandings of the term 'Asian' relate to ethnic groups from places such as China and Vietnam. In the mid-1980s, opposition to Asian immigration persisted. However, the arguments against it were more sophisticated than those mounted in the post-war period. A comment attributed to the first minister for immigration, Arthur Calwell, that 'two wongs don't make a white', has become part of the mythology surrounding the immigration policies of the post-war period, premised as these were on the White Australia Policy (Department of Immigration and Ethnic Affairs 1986; Secretariat to the Committee to Advise on Australia's Immigration Policies 1987; Foster 1988). None the less, more recent opposition still used Asian appearance and particular cultural traits to argue their non-belonging in Australian society.

In 1984, a debate on Asian immigration focused on arguments made by the conservative historian, Professor Blainey. He focused on Australia's ability to integrate refugees created by the Vietnam war. He argued that Australian society could not accommodate a large number of refugees who were so culturally and physically different in the time-frame proposed, without this constituting a threat to social cohesion. The argument was also expounded in relation to the well-being of the refugees. Given the assumed hostility towards them from the existing population, the argument was made that it would be inhumane to allow them to enter in the numbers and time-frame being proposed (Blainey 1984; Cope and Morrissey 1986; Castles *et al.* 1988; Office of the Minister of Ethnic Affairs undated).

So, for example, the concern was not whether Chinese-Vietnamese refugees fleeing the consequences of the Vietnam war would integrate with the Chinese-Australian population which had been in Australia since the Gold Rushes, it was a matter of whether the ethnic majority would feel comfortable with the so-called Asianization of Australian streetscapes. Again, Asian physical features were highlighted to demark exclusion because the desired end-point was the maintenance of the existing Australian hegemony, defined in terms of its Britishness. The debate in the 1980s also focused on work practices associated with the would-be immigrants. In relation to the refugees from Vietnam and its surrounding region, questions were raised about their lack of union experience and the threat this could pose to Australian working conditions and industrial rights (Cope and Morrissey 1986; Castles *et al.* 1988; Office of the Minister of Ethnic Affairs undated).

Increasingly, however, the relationship between Australia and Asia is being shaped by new economic directions within the region. The desire to compete for a market share within some Asian economies, has framed more recent discourses surrounding Australian–Asian relations. This has created a paradoxical situation whereby traditional conceptions of Asia are having to be reconciled with new imperatives, often through public discourses related to national development and citizenship. Rizvi (1996) makes the point that since the Second World War, Australian representations of Asia have become more complex and contradictory as there are attempts to reconcile the new economic order in the region and Australia's place within this. He states:

Australians are now keenly aware of their location in the Asia-Pacific region, but find it difficult to discard the earlier racist images of Asia. They recognise Asia as inextricably linked to their critical and political objectives, but are unable to secure sufficient distance from the racial stereotyping that involved viewing Asians as a homogenised mass who posed a constant threat to Australia's national identity and to its economic well-being.

(Rizvi 1996: 178)

In Australia, racialization remains clearest in relation to the Aboriginal peoples and those considered Asian. None the less, these groups are not the only ones to experience some form of racialization. Physical features such as skin colour and hair type have been used in a process of racialization which has seen other groups experience most severe forms of exclusion, often linked to immigration policy. The notions of racial purity, discussed above, were also used in relation to southern European immigrants who were understood as inferior to the Australian type. White (1985) provides an example of the vitriol against Italian immigrants published in *Smith's Weekly* which referred to them as 'that greasy flood of Mediterranean scum that seeks to defile and debase Australia' (White 1985: 141). *Smith's Weekly* was a populist newspaper owned by a Sydney entrepreneur who was later to become Lord Mayor of the city. The paper, which was published between the wars had a reputation for larrikinism – an anti-establishment spirit – albeit from a right-wing political stance (Blaikie 1979).

Non-British immigration to Australia has a long history. In relation to groups associated with southern Europe this has been characterized by avoidance. Quotas have been variously set and at times immigration from this region has been disallowed. The White Australia Policy has been enacted in relation to would-be immigrants not currently racialized. For example, Maltese and Cypriots have been denied entry to Australia on the basis of their skin colour, even though they were British subjects at the time (London 1970; York 1990). While such groups, at this point in time, are not necessarily racialized, this is a product of social and historical circumstances rather than an immutable fact. These ethnic groups are susceptible to racialization and this is illustrated by the fact that at other points in Australian history, this has occurred.

Sentiments such as those from *Smith's Weekly*, variously framed as defilement, inferiority or incompatibility, lay at the foundation of Australia's post-war immigration programme. It was through this programme, the intention of which was to increase the population dramatically and quickly, that the rhetoric of 'race' gave way to that of ethnicity (de Lepervanche 1980). Social Darwinism, together with its quest for human classification, was met with pronounced scepticism within the social sciences after the Second World War and the horrors of the extermination camps. None the less, there was a clear understanding in Australia of what constituted 'Australian' and the 'Australian way of life'. This was reflected in the explicit government preference for British immigrants. When such immigrants failed to come in the desired numbers, despite incentives such as assisted passage schemes which made the cost of travel minimal, the government set about consolidating a hierarchy of desirability. This coincided with familiarity, often established on the basis of physical features. For example, people from northern Europe were deemed more desirable because of their blonde hair, blue eyes and fair complexions. Cultural traits were also important in relation to determining the possibility of successful assimilation. As the government grew more desperate for immigrants, the source countries became more diverse. It was in this context of 'least desirable' that so many people from southern Europe entered Australia to become 'factory fodder' in its rapid industrialization.

Whilst racism has taken many forms, the emphasis on sameness as a prerequisite for compatibility continues. In Australia this has been traditionally framed through political discourses related to assimilation. At various points in time, groups such as the southern Europeans and Asians have been considered naturally incompatible with the Australian way of life because of a range of presumed physical and cultural attributes. Muslim groups have also been highlighted as not belonging; their dress and therefore appearance, as well as cultural practices associated with their religion, have been used to demark exclusion and natural non-belonging (Human Rights and Equal Opportunity Commission 1991; Victorian Committee to Advise the Attorney-General on Racial Vilification 1992).

It is also important to consider that this sense of non-belonging may not be linked in straightforward ways to chronology. It is popularly considered that 'newness' and unfamiliarity are the causes of racism. Minority groups remain vulnerable and we can consider this through the experiences of German and Italo-Australians who were interned during the First and Second World Wars despite Australian residency and citizenship. David Suzuki, the Canadian environmentalist, attributes his interest in genetics to the fact that he and his parents were interned during the Second World War because they were considered Japanese and therefore a threat to the state. Up until that point, Suzuki had never considered himself other than Canadian (Suzuki and Oiwa 1996).

More recently in Australia, there is the case of what has been described as a witch-hunt among the Greek community of Sydney in the 1980s. Bottomley (1992) describes the Commonwealth police dawn raids on the homes of Greek patients of doctors suspected of fraud. Approximately 184 people were arrested and jailed. Later, close to 800 pensioners had their benefits suspended. Bottomley (1992) outlines the consequences of this harassment and abuse of civil liberties which has included reported suicides and long-term traumas. After four years of legal proceedings, all charges were dropped. Bottomley concludes:

There is no doubt that such mass raids could not have been made on English or American migrants, or on super-wealthy Anglophone tax avoiders (who *do* exist). The evidence suggests that this was a lesson to discourage 'ethnics' from the potential misuse of the welfare system.

(Bottomley 1992: 159, original emphasis)

One of the strongest indices of perceived in/compatibility is an ethnic group's propensity for maintaining its difference. A capacity to maintain difference is often considered through indices related to mother-tongue maintenance and out-marriage. If one considers marriage, family and child-rearing as heavily feminized domains, the significance of the relationship between cultural difference and gender becomes manifest.

## Gender and ethnic boundary making and breaking

The important role played by gender in the demarcation of ethnic boundaries needs to be considered. There has been a sustained examination of this relationship by Anthias and Yuval-Davis (1983; Yuval-Davis and Anthias 1989; Yuval-Davis and Werbner 1999). In summary, they state:

The boundary of the ethnic is often dependent on gender and there is a reliance on gender attributes for specifying ethnic identity; much of ethnic culture is organized around rules relating to sexuality, marriage and the family, and a true member will perform these roles properly. Communal boundaries often use differences in the way women are socially constructed as markers. Such markers (for example, expectations about honour, purity, the mothering of patriots, reproducers of the nation, transmitters of ethnic culture) often symbolize the use of women as an ethnic resource.

(Anthias and Yuval-Davis 1992: 114)

Not only can ethnicity depend on gender attributes being played out correctly, but also the desire to maintain ethnic difference can result in the policing of women and their sexuality. This is a complex dynamic that impacts on minority women from within their collectivities as well as from the mainstream society. In this way, it is a two-way dynamic, interrelated and mutually dependent, growing out of and in turn influencing how the minority views the majority and the how the majority views the minority.

The complexity and impact of this dynamic can be more burdensome for minority women. The experience of racism makes these collectivities sources of support and comfort. None the less, a 'state of siege' mentality resulting from experiences of racism, can increase the relevance and importance of the ethnic collectivity and this can place an increased pressure on minority women, given their pivotal role in the maintenance of ethnic boundaries.

The maintenance of such boundaries also impacts on majority women. This is possibly clearest in relation to arguments concerned with racial purity and the need for women to be 'breeders of the white race'. In Australia around the beginning of the twentieth century, there was a concern that the so-called Anglo-Saxon 'race' would not survive. The white birthrate was in decline and this was considered an outcome of women becoming educated and emancipated. There also existed an understanding that the threat to racial purity was exacerbated by Asian and Pacific men who immigrated to Australia prior to the introduction of the White Australia Policy. These men were considered a threat to 'virtuous white women'. This concern with 'race suicide' resurfaced in 1912 when Aboriginal and 'Asian' women were not granted the maternity allowance and (in the 1920s) child endowment. In both cases, monetary incentives were used to exhort white women to do their 'natural duty' so that the breeding gap between black and white 'races' could be closed (McQueen 1986; de Lepervanche 1989).

Gender has also operated as an ethnic marker in relation to southern European immigrants. After the Second World War, Australian government policy at particular periods was to encourage female migration to Australia. Young, single women were brought to Australia, on what have been termed 'brideships', as partners for the disproportionate number of single men from their regions of origin who had already immigrated. These single men were conceived of as a potential threat to ethnic majority women and also more likely to create trouble in the absence of what has been understood as the civilizing influence of women. The creation of nuclear family units was understood to bestow the benefits of sexual gratification and the disciplining implications of having responsibility for children. Moreover, such units would assist with the creation of maximum industrial efficiency through female immigrants providing men with the support needed to become good workers (Branson and Miller 1979; Martin 1984; Kunek 1993).

Anthias and Yuval-Davis (1983) stress the importance of relations between the sexes in the creation of an ethnic identity. However, they also stress not only that these practices are internal to the ethnic collectivities but also that gender roles are used to specify ethnic difference by outsiders, as in racial stereotypes concerned with the patriarchal Asian father or the black sexual 'stud' (Anthias and Yuval-Davis 1983). The exploration of the role that gender plays in characterizing ethnicity, both within the collectivity and by outsiders in relation to it, is a theme explored at great length by many antiracist feminists. In particular, there is concern to explore representations of gender relations within minority communities relative to the experience of these gender relations by minority women (Sykes 1975; hooks 1981; Parmar 1982; Anzaldua 1987; Collins 1990; Huggins 1991; Brah 1996).

Implicit in 'them and us' divides are concepts of inferiority and superiority, of boundaries being necessary in order to keep what is deemed superior distinct. Within racist ideologies, gender relations have been used as a measure of civilization and a justification for intervention. For example, relations between Aboriginal women and men as they were understood by colonizing men, steeped in the gender relations of Georgian England, were used to justify their estimation of the indigenous people's near-animal status and on this basis their attempted genocide and ethnocide (Hamilton 1975; White 1985; Hughes 1988).

More recently, the dominant assumption about Aboriginal women's invisibility and lack of agency has come to the forefront in legal procedures in relation to land claims. White institutional practices, assuming patriarchal models, have been blind to aspects of Aboriginal women's cultures and in this way failed to adequately recognize Aboriginal women as landowners and involve them in the full breadth of proceedings (Bird Rose 1996).

The use of gender relations to establish and maintain hierarchies of civilization has been challenged by antiracist feminists (El Sadaawi 1980; Davis 1981; hooks 1984; Anzaldua 1987; Phoenix 1990; Huggins 1991). These feminists have questioned the understanding implicit in such hierarchies, that for minority women, it is their home culture rather than mainstream society, which is the major cause of their oppression. They have also highlighted the fact that within such characterizations, minority women are created as objects, their voices and histories of struggle against both sexism and racism, remaining silenced.

Gender relations are inextricably linked to the demarking of ethnicity. It is through the family in particular that these relations are played out and given meaning. It is not surprising, then, that the family has become a major site for debates between feminists as to the significance of difference. Since the late 1970s, feminist movements have been confronted with the contradictions implicit in campaigns around seemingly universal issues. Issues as fundamental to feminism as the family, birth control and rape have been problematized by antiracist feminists who reinterpret mainstream understandings of these in relation to their experience and theorization of racism (Sykes 1975; El Sadaawi 1980; Davis 1981; hooks 1981; Bligh 1983; Smith 1990). Such feminists have provided nuanced interpretations of the role of gender in ethnic boundary making and racialization which strike at the heart of essentialist interpretations of what it means to be a woman.

In the Australian context, these developments have been articulated in relation to Aboriginal women and minority women ( Bottomley *et al.* 1991; Pettman 1992; Huggins and Saunders 1993). In relation to those ethnic minority communities which are least likely to experience racialization, gender relations, perhaps more than anything else, have been consistently understood to create the 'them and us' divide. In his discussion of southern Europeans in Australia, Price (1963) stressed gender relations, so much so that he considers these to be the fundamental reason for these groups' unsuccessful assimilation. Price argued that there is a fundamental difference between the degree to which women from 'our particular districts of origin' and women from Greece and southern Italy and southern Spain are 'permitted to pursue social and business activities outside the home' (Price 1963: 59). He contends, in relation to the latter, that there is a view that if a man and a woman are left alone together they will 'inevitably make love. Consequently unmarried girls were not allowed out unless strictly chaperoned, nor might an unaccompanied married woman walk or talk with any man not her husband' (Price 1963: 59). It would be comforting to accept this interpretation as a product of a period in Australian history dominated by the discourses of assimilation. However, one of the intentions here is to examine how this view has extended beyond the time-frame of assimilation and into the more progressive discourses related to multiculturalism and gender equity. Particular emphasis will be given to such discourses as they relate to schooling in following chapters.

Black and ethnic minority women experience a range of articulated oppressions. In such a context, an analysis of their situation which focuses on their family or home culture needs to be considered carefully. Many feminists have argued against the pathologizing of black families and instead have created a case for why, in light of racism, their families may function as sources of support rather than simply oppression (Boyle 1983; Collins 1990; hooks 1990; Phoenix 1990; Huggins 1991; Brah 1996). Parallels can be drawn between this argument and the Australian situation in relation to ethnicity, most specifically in this context, those labelled southern European. In relation to southern European communities, it is not unusual for an emphasis to be placed on family structures seen to reflect backward, quasi-feudal conditions which exist in the industrially undeveloped communities within the country of origin. It is the transposition of these structures into the Australian context which is seen to create problems. Hence, there is an emphasis in literature dealing with Australian southern European ethnic minority women and girls, on features which are understood to characterize the communities in their countries of origin; features such as the small farm-based economies, dowries, arranged marriages and the chaperoning of women. These issues are referred to in the Australian situation, even in relation to women and girls born in Australia (Price 1963; Bottomley 1984; Strinzos 1984; Kalantzis 1987).

## Ethnic minority women: their status in Australia

The period between 1950 and 1974 has been considered a boom period in terms of economic growth in Australia. There was a rapid increase in population, industrialization, personal expenditure and suburban development, particularly in Melbourne and Sydney. In this period the population grew from 8.3 million to 13.6 million, with immigration contributing approximately half of this increase. Manufacturing industry expanded and between

1961 and 1975 the labour force grew by 1.8 million people. Part of this growth was due, not to an increase in population size, but to the increased number of women in the labour force. Between 1954 and 1966 the number of women in the labour force had increased by 70 per cent and by 1974 65 per cent of women in the labour force were married. A significant element in this increase was the number of immigrant women who had joined the Australian labour force, with a participation rate of 49.3 per cent for those married. Relative to Australian-born women, these women were disproportionately represented in the new manufacturing industries which required unskilled workers (Women's Bureau, Department of Employment and Youth Affairs 1981).

Moreover, women from southern European countries were concentrated in labouring and process work. During this period, 45 per cent of women born in Italy, 56 per cent of women born in Greece and 54 per cent of women born in Yugoslavia were in these areas relative to 9.2 per cent of Australian-born women, 14.2 per cent of women born in the British Isles and 20 per cent of the women born in Germany (Storer undated: 2). In 1975 the Jackson Committee established to advise the government on policies for manufacturing industry highlighted these women's situation by stating that:

> The workforce is multi-racial and multi-cultural. Four out of 10 are born outside Australia. They most frequently do the dirtiest, least skilled, menial tasks; tasks for which, despite unemployment, young native-born Australians cannot be found. Women are a quarter of the workforce and in some sectors 8 out of 10. Little attention is paid to their special needs, particularly of the two-thirds who are married. The married migrant woman in industry is trebly disadvantaged.
> (Women's Bureau, Department of Employment and Youth Affairs 1981: 5)

This disadvantage was elaborated in detail in a study conducted by the Centre for Urban Research and Action (CURA) in Melbourne with its investigation of immigrant women in industry. The report from this research, entitled *'But I Wouldn't Want My Wife to Work Here . . .'* (Storer undated), highlighted how little research had been carried out in the area prior to this study (Storer undated: 3).

Despite having been published in the mid-1970s, this report is highlighted as significant here for several reasons. Coinciding with the International Year of Women, it was a very lonely attempt to consider the experiences of this group of women. I would argue that the work it started was inadequately considered and continued within mainstream feminism at the time. I have argued elsewhere (Tsolidis 1990) that issues surrounding minority women in Australia have been taken up through movements concerned with ethnic rights more so than within the women's movement and this is a similar case in point.

Perhaps more importantly, the experiences of these women and the attitudes expressed towards them form a fundamental backdrop for the ways they and their daughters are considered today. In following sections of the chapter I shall argue that the representation of minority women, specifically those from southern Europe, are informed by the conditions they endured during the 1970s and 1980s. Although economic restructuring may have altered the character of work and following this, patterns of immigration, these women's experiences and what motivated them, linger negatively in the public imagination and positively in the minds of their children, many of whom now express this through literary endeavours (Gunew and Longley 1992; Kamboureli 1996).

The CURA report developed a picture of southern European immigrant women enduring poorly paid, repetitive work for reasons of economic survival and in anticipation of providing their children with better opportunities. Its findings highlighted the lack of adequate child-care, their need for English language tuition, their neglect by unions and their intense dislike for the poor conditions and humiliating treatment they experience.

In summary this study found that most of these women had not worked in factories prior to coming to Australia and that in their countries of origin had come from small villages where they worked on farms, in the village or in the home. The majority had had minimal education and could not speak English. Most were married to unskilled or semi-skilled men, were between 25 and 45 years of age with between one and three children. The study found that the more recent immigrants were in the 'dirtiest' industries such as the meat industry and that those who had been in Australia for longer periods were in 'cleaner' industries such as the clothing industry.

The report outlined the poor physical conditions in the factories and the humiliating work systems these immigrant women faced. These included extreme regimentation to the point of being timed in the toilet and bonus systems designed to maximize production. While 80 per cent of the women involved in the study stated that they worked for reasons of economic survival, rather than list low wages as their major complaint, they instead stressed the inhumanity of the systems they worked under.

The report highlighted the fact that 80 per cent of the women in the study had not received any English language tuition despite the fact that 90 per cent stated that they would attend classes if these were provided at work, 74 per cent wanted their unions to act on this issue and 40 per cent stated that they were willing to strike over the issue (Storer undated: 111). Similarly, 73 per cent of the women involved in the study stated that their unions should work for adequate child-care, an issue that the report highlighted as a major concern for these women. Despite this, the report also highlighted the poor relationship between these women and their unions.

Almost a decade later, a similar pattern emerged. In 1983 married immigrant women had a higher participation rate in the labour force than

Australian-born women, this being particularly so for southern European women. They were still over-represented in labouring and process work which attracted the lowest rates of pay. However, during this period unemployment rates were also an element within the picture, unlike the post-war boom period, and immigrant women also experienced a higher rate of unemployment than Australian-born women. Similar concerns in relation to child-care still existed with immigrant women forced to use care arrangements for their children with which they were clearly dissatisfied and there was still an unmet need for workplace child-care provision (Pankhurst 1984).

Figures for 1989 indicated that immigrant women from non-English-speaking countries were still over-represented in labouring and process work: 34.8 per cent of these women were employed in such positions, compared with 13.7 per cent of non-immigrant women and 18 per cent of immigrant women from English-speaking countries. Similarly, the most recently arrived immigrants were concentrated in the most dangerous of manufacturing industries (Alcorso and Schofield 1991). At the beginning of the 1990s the picture which had emerged in the mid-1970s of immigrant women being one of the most disadvantaged sections of the Australian labour force remained little altered. Moreover, the long-term effects of this status began to emerge clearly.

A study concerning the health of non-English-speaking background women indicated that, as a group, they had been severely handicapped by their work-history in Australia. The National Non-English Speaking Background Women's Health Strategy (Alcorso and Schofield 1991) argued that non-English-speaking background women had higher rates of work-related illnesses and injuries and a greater incidence of poor mental and emotional health conditions. Moreover, it drew a clear link between this and migration, arguing that these women's health deteriorated with their length of residency in Australia. While these women came to Australia with a generally higher level of health than that of Australian-born women and those born in English-speaking countries, this declined with Australian residency independently of factors related to ageing.

These women, particularly the longer-term residents, namely those from southern Europe, experienced a higher rate of employment-related injuries and poor mental and emotional health conditions. The strategy linked this health deterioration with the work conditions in Australian manufacturing industries, their lack of English proficiency and lack of familiarity with work processes and products. A link was also made between their poor mental and emotional health and the pressures related to migration. For example, these women experienced severe alienation and had the added responsibility of caring for family members in isolation from familiar networks. In short, the strategy highlighted the consequences of the disadvantages which immigrant women faced in Australia and to which the CURA report drew attention almost fifteen years previously. These disadvantages continue to be highlighted (Bottomley *et al.* 1991; Pettman 1992).

### Southern European women: representations

For the southern European women who migrated to Australia in the post-war period, the picture that emerges is one of extreme oppression. Married and with children, they joined the labour force in larger proportions than Australian-born women, they have been concentrated in labouring and process work in manufacturing industry, and more so in sections of such industries where Australian-born women, even in times of unemployment, have refused to work. The work they have undertaken has been poorly paid, dirty, repetitive and dangerous, to the extent that there have been significant health repercussions for these women. The work processes they have experienced have been designed to maximize production at the cost of these women's dignity, physical and mental health. They have had urgent and unmet needs, particularly in the areas of child-care and English language tuition, and their unions have failed to advocate on their behalf. Moreover, migration has isolated them from networks of support and increased the burdens on them in relation to caring for other family members. While the position they occupy in the Australian labour force and the social and economic consequences of the migration process have been given as an explanation for the disadvantage they experience (Storer undated; Pankhurst 1984; Alcorso and Schofield 1991; Bottomley *et al.* 1991; Pettman 1992), there is none the less a view that the position they occupy within Australian society is a consequence of factors considered 'natural' rather than social, or which result from 'their cultures' rather than from their position in Australian society.

This view is obvious in the comments made by employers interviewed as part of the CURA study. In general terms they considered the southern European women they employed as somehow 'naturally' suited to the poor conditions, repetitive work and humiliating work practices in their factories because they were both immigrants and women. These employers were clearly of the opinion that southern European women were best suited to factory work and voiced a suspicion of Australian-born workers who applied for similar work because competent Australians would not seek such work. Some employers stated that women were more dextrous and therefore suitable to the type of manual work they made available. Others said specifically of southern European women that they were better able to cope with jobs which required them to repeat the same action hundreds of times a day. These employers argued that southern European women worked harder than Australian workers because they were desperate or greedy; that is, on arriving in Australia they needed money to establish themselves or to buy the goods that were now available to them. Some explained that the bonus system was used to capitalize on this incentive and make the women work harder and faster.

The cultural backgrounds of these women were also used to explain their suitability to the work conditions they experienced. Comments were made about their 'primitive' backgrounds and their suitability to, and even enjoyment of, hard, repetitive work. For example, employers commented:

It's not hard work. I get no complaints. It's an ideal job for women to do because there's nothing skilful or hard in it.

The women are suited to these jobs because they can sit at the machine all day doing the same thing. If they were more intelligent or better educated they would become bored or go round the bend. But this class of person is suited to the job. These women come from peasant type backgrounds.

It's not hard physically. It is mentally tedious work but that doesn't seem to worry them. They know no different.

(Storer undated: 82)

Despite the obviously oppressive nature of the work which these employers were clearly aware of (in fact the title of the report, *'But I Wouldn't Want my Wife to Work Here . . .'*, is based on a comment by one such employer) they none the less felt that factors related to southern European women's backgrounds explained the disadvantage they experienced. Along with comments related to their intelligence, primitive backgrounds and lack of education, employers also commented on their status within their communities and families. They understood these women to be poorly treated by domineering husbands and felt that they were passive and accepting of this with no interest in women's rights. For example, one commented that these women 'are like sheep. They are led by their husbands' (Storer undated: 86). Others argued that these women were work-fatigued because of the home duties they were expected to perform. Other comments included:

Migrant women are pretty unliberated. Many give their pay packet to their husbands. And they have to go home, cook and clean, and don't finish till 10 pm. Certainly it's a two job situation.

Their customs are male oriented. For instance, the Yugoslav women stand behind their men and don't sit down to have their meal until the men finish. Women are often regarded as chattels in their own home.

A lot of these women have a husband who is a boozer, wayward and a gambler. Where can these women go? They would be considered bad women in their society for leaving. They come to work fatigued.

(Storer undated: 87)

This issue is dealt with in some detail here because it is a stark example of the relationship between the representation of women from southern European communities and gender relations within these communities relative to the lived reality of these women. The women interviewed for the CURA study presented a vastly different picture of their situation from that presented by the men quoted above. They were disgruntled with their work conditions, primarily because of the ways in which they were treated, and foremost in this regard, they discussed the discrimination they experienced in relations with management and fellow-workers. They highlighted their need for appropriate child-care, English-language tuition and union advocacy.

The argument developed here is that the current situation for women and girls from these communities needs to be considered in relation to the dominant representations of their communities. The understandings of their communities and the women who are their mothers and grandmothers, exemplified by these employers' comments, are their legacy. While positions of the daughters and granddaughters of the women who immigrated in the post-war period may have altered, the representations of their communities and the gender relations which operate within them, is little altered. Martin (1996) in her discussion of media representations comments: 'Most commonly, non-Anglo-Australian women are represented in servant roles, or as fat, comical, earth-mommas serving their marginal "families"' (Martin 1996: 147). Two examples will be discussed here to illustrate this point.

Mark Mitchell is an Australian comedian who, during the 1980s and 1990s, depicted the character of 'Con the Fruiter'. Con is a Greek greengrocer who is married to Marika, also played by Mitchell. They have several daughters, Voula, Toula, Roula and Soula, who are, significantly, referred to but seldom if ever seen. Both Con and Marika are extreme of girth, have abundant facial hair and speak in the way often presumed of working-class Greek immigrants; that is, with a heavy accent, ungrammatical, broken English delivered with exaggerated hand gestures. They are depicted as childlike and unsophisticated. Moreover, what is meant to make these characters amusing, especially Marika, is their simple, non-nuanced understandings of life in Australia and their almost pathetic appreciation of the lifestyle that is the product of their migration. Mitchell initially introduced the characterization of Con and Marika through television comedy shows. Increasingly, however, these characters are seen in a range of advertisements. In one such advertisement, Marika is depicted being ordered by her husband to jump off a truck in order to level a pile of cardboard boxes. Represented through this advertisement are a range of understandings related to Greek women in this instance, but which are common in relation to southern Europeans more generally; that is, their embodiment, their relations with dominant husbands, fathers or brothers and their lack of agency and resistance. These issues will be discussed further.

While it may not surprise us that Mark Mitchell does not base his characterizations on sophisticated feminist understandings, this image of southern European communities is evident in other work, from which we may expect more. In an article for *The Age* newspaper, Beatrice Faust (1993), an outspoken feminist writer and academic, addressed the issue of multiculturalism. In particular she expounded the idea that multiculturalism is an ephemeral concept which serves the purposes of the self-seeking 'second-generation migrants'. These are the daughters and sons of hard-working immigrants who asked for little and instead were thankful for the opportunity to toil in Australian factories and schemes such as that at the Snowy Mountains, where immigrants were expected to work constructing a hydro-electricity project as a condition of migration.

> Who wanted multiculturalism? Not the men of the Snowy Mountains Project. Not the kneaders of pasta and pourers of terrazzo, not the cheerful corner-shop keepers. During the 1950s and even into the 1980s, it was still possible to envisage prosperity through hard work – the goal was not cultural recognition from the WASP majority but meat every day and eventually a three-limousine wedding with a 20-tier wedding cake for the daughters . . .The children of this hard-working generation became the multiculturalists, capitalising on their ethnic origins to gain a fast-track into the dominant middle-class. They sometimes took their background and the difficulty of their parents' lives as subject matter but the voices, the visions and the value-systems were not breathtakingly inventive.
>
> (Faust 1993)

Faust's invective is directed against the notion of diversified understandings of cultural worth and she states that the children of immigrants, those who identify with multiculturalism, show a 'contempt for culture itself' and use their ethnic origins simply as a device to 'fast-track into the dominant middle-class'. Implicit in her article is the idea that 'ethnics' do not need special consideration because they are doing better than their parents for a lot less effort and this should make them happy enough.

The understanding that 'Australian' equals 'ethnic majority' is clear in Faust's article. However, what is of particular interest here is that she shares her understanding of what it means to be southern European with Mark Mitchell. Again we have a reference to the 'cheerful' corner-shop owner and prosperity through hard labour which assumes the hands and not the mind. Importantly, also, one of the aims of this prosperity is the ability to provide daughters with ostentatious weddings. Again, like the mostly faceless Roula, Toula and Soula who are Con and Marika's daughters, Faust denies these daughters' agency and harks back to the commonsense understandings of gender relations within such communities – those reminiscent of arranged marriages, dowries and village celebrations.

Perhaps one of the most noteworthy aspects of Faust's argument is her denigration of the cultural output of these so-called career multiculturalists. Within Australia, as elsewhere, there has been an ongoing effort to redefine the hegemonic through the inclusion of minority experience in the arts. The argument is made that it is not 'migrant' literature, for example, but Australian literature, and that the inclusion of minority experience in this way challenges dominant understandings of what it means to be Australian. Additionally, it exposes the existing criteria for artistic merit as culturally situated in itself (Gunew and Rizvi 1994). Faust maintains that 'good' culture is culture that meets long-established standards without considering such standards as mechanisms for maintaining existing hegemonies. Instead, she argues that multiculturalists have uninventive output and expect to succeed despite this. It seems that within such a framework we are left only with the Mark Mitchell depictions of minorities and the substandard ones produced by career multiculturalists!

Such representations of ethnic minority women, their communities and gender relations within them, must be considered also in light of how infrequently such women and communities enter the media. In fact, in the Australian context, cultural difference is minimally represented particularly on television. By and large, ethnic diversity remains within the confines of print media, radio and television specifically designed to cater for minority communities. Outside this, particularly with regard to television, diversity is due more to regulations in existence in the USA which allow blacks to enter our homes through programmes in which they feature (Goodall *et al.* 1991). In this context, the impact of the Soulas, Roulas, Toulas, Marikas and Cons on the public imagination is ever more poignant, as are the debates about the so-called career multiculturalists and the worth of their cultural output.

The less than flattering depiction of their bodies is something that young women from southern European communities face and react against through severe dieting or exercise programmes, bleaching, plucking and waxing. It is often also reinforced through men in their communities who adhere to dominant images of female attractiveness. It is a complicated and convoluted self-hate, mediated by unequal relations within and between the categories of ethnicity and gender, which infiltrates sexual attraction to the Other. This issue is inextricably linked to the relationship between racism and phallocentrism (hooks 1992).

As Bill the Grozzer illustrates at the start of this chapter, his wife and the woman who could have been his wife represent through their embodiment his choice between the minority and the mainstream. While both the redhead and the brunette are constructed as acted upon, as choices rather than choosers, the red-head is linked with upward social mobility. The brunette, on the other hand, is the fall-back, albeit potentially happy, choice. This is further illustrated in the story by the fact that Toula is now married to a Grozzer who had an unsuccessful marriage with an 'Australian'. Bill had no difficulty telling which of this Grozzer's two children was mothered by Toula and which by his first wife.

> He was the taller of the two, white-skinned with light brown hair; his brother was black-haired, had an olive complexion and strangely a much larger head.
>
> (Athanasou 1995: 332)

While all women have to develop a sense of aesthetics in contradistinction to phallocentric images of womanhood, for minority women this is further complicated by processes of othering. Not only do they have to redefine themselves against the grain of natural attributes such as body shape and colouring, but also such attributes are taken to represent a range of cultural positionings related to sexuality; for example, Latin sensuality and peasant earthiness. In the case of Australian southern European women, these most commonly presume the representations expounded by Price (1963), quoted above. Those related to being over-protected because they are incapable of making judgements about their own sexuality. In the context of majority–minority power relations we are faced with the distinction between the sophisticated, refined, urban, liberated and cerebral and the rural, earthy, sensual and in need of containment; in summary the distinction between the civilized and uncivilized at the core of understandings of cultures as hierarchical. The age-old dilemma for women between the virgin and the vixen or in Summer's (1975) terms, the damned whore or God's police, needs to be considered as it is ethnicized. As I shall be arguing in later chapters, within secondary schooling during adolescence, processes of identification are inextricably linked to ethnicity, gender and, as part of this, sexuality.

The experiences and representations of the minority women described here are not those of a bygone era. Many women from this region still work in similar conditions and the aspirations they have for their children are based on the hope that their children will escape similar fates. Similarly, the representations of these communities, and the gender relations within them, remain and influence the ways in which teachers consider such parents, their attitudes towards their children and how teachers consider the children themselves as their students (Tsolidis 1986).

Given the concern here with education, the aim is to draw on the above discussion and relate it to ethnic minority girls and schooling more specifically. This will be done initially, through a reading of policy dealing with cultural difference or gender equity. Within policy concerned with the education of girls, has equality and difference been considered as it applies within the category 'girls'? On the other hand, with regard to multicultural policy, has gender equity been considered in the context of difference?

# 3 Equality OR difference: representations of ethnic minority girls in education policy

I have argued that ethnic minority groups, including those not commonly racialized, experience their Australianness as perpetual transience, caught up in the discourses of non-belonging which distinguish 'real' and 'non-real' Australians. I also argued that compatibility, understood as sameness, is judged through a range of indices which foreground the significance of gender. The intention in this chapter is to examine education policy concerned with either multiculturalism or gender equity and read it in relation to these understandings. The intention is to consider the articulation of gender and ethnicity within such discourses as a means of understanding political strategies which variously privilege equity or difference. Additionally, the intention is to draw some strategic possibilities out of such policies as a way forward.

The policies deemed most relevant here are those dealing with gender equity and those dealing with multiculturalism. Not only should these policies be the most relevant given that they deal with gender and cultural difference between them, but also they represent a means of exploring equity and difference in broader terms. In the Australian context, most typically, multiculturalism has a strong association with the type of pluralism not commonly concerned with equity. On the other hand, gender equity policy is traditionally associated with an understanding of equity, which has a limited engagement with difference. The aim is to read these policies for their positioning of ethnic minority girls as a means of casting some light on how equity and difference can be understood in relation to each other.

The policies to be considered were produced over a 20-year period. During this time there were changes of government and shifts in priorities which reflected evolving social and economic realities and political responses to these. In some ways these shifts in context serve to highlight the relative consistency in approach regarding the representation of ethnic minority women and girls.

It is important to acknowledge that most of the policy considered here is reformist in intent. By and large, it grew out of or was framed by a period of optimism with regard to the possibility of change. As discussed in the introductory chapter of this book, the late 1970s and early 1980s were times when teachers were initiating changes related to school-based and student-centred curriculum, pedagogy and assessment. At a general level within Australian education and particularly within the State of Victoria, this optimism was characterized by a shift away from compensatory models, to those which problematized the curriculum instead of the groups of students mainstream curriculum had traditionally alienated. Much of this movement, particularly in relation to gender equity, fell under the rubric of inclusive curriculum (Yates 1987). This shift away from models which assumed a deficit understanding of so-called disadvantaged students is particularly relevant to this exercise. One of the aims is to explore whether the more progressive curriculum models offer ethnic minority girls a framework for a more equitable schooling experience. Have such models gone some way towards both recognizing the specificity of their experience as well as giving them access to the full range of academic, social and career possibilities? Have such models gone some way towards resolving the commonly constructed tension between equity and difference?

A traditional framework for the consideration of such questions is that of 'culture clash'. It bespeaks the neat separation between the 'them and us' that has dominated analyses of ethnic minority students. The relative compassion shown for the students caught in this 'culture clash' may differ and the strategies to ameliorate their transition from the 'them' to the 'us' may differ, but commonly there is little debate about the fact that the 'them' needs to become like the 'us'. Not only is this 'usness' good for society, but also it is good for the 'them' given the assumed superiority of the 'us'. Within the 'culture clash' model there is often specific concern for girls. Ethnic minority girls, it is understood, suffer the consequences of this situation more so than their brothers. This is because gender relations within their communities are understood to be less urbane, less emancipatory and less comfortable for them as girls. This is one exemplar of the issues discussed in Chapter 2 with regard to the role of gender relations in demarking, maintaining and potentially assimilating difference.

What are the policy discourses, which frame and reflect the ways in which ethnic minority girls are understood? If we understand policy to reflect one particular set of meanings, in this case about the articulation of gender and ethnicity, can we remake these meanings by placing them alongside an alternative set of meanings?

I would like to explore these questions in relation to two issues. First, the policies related to gender equity and multiculturalism discussed here, by and large, grew out of a reformist period brought about the election of a Labor government in Australia and in the State of Victoria, after a very long time of conservative rule. In this context, such policies reflected social movements concerned with feminism and ethnic rights respectively. The reading of gender equity and multicultural policies against each other, in order to position ethnic minority girls as subjects, is my attempt to reflect what Yeatman (1994) refers to as a 'non-consensualist politics of difference'. This is a politics which does not attempt an homogenous identity. Participants make no claim to common culture but instead 'continually reinterpret the movement and its goals in relation to the changing character of their own personal histories' (Yeatman, 1994: 119). With reference to feminist movement specifically, Yeatman argues that there exists an internal politics of difference. She argues for differentiated speaking locations, 'as many as there are discursively posited differences among women (Yeatman, 1994: 120). In this way, an alternative reading of gender equity policy which attempts to draw out the ethnic minority 'voice' is a reflection of a politics of difference within feminism. In relation to most multicultural policy, it represents a feminist incursion.

The second issue I wish to draw attention to in exploring questions about the role of policy, is the possibility that an alternative set of meanings can be provided from ethnic minority girls. Voicing silences and having the right to speak are concepts most familiar within feminism, as evidenced by the opening of this book! With regard to ethnic minority school girls, the aim is to provide their perspective on a range of relevant issues as an alternative set of meanings which may allow us to review and remake the dominant educational discourses about them. Their perspectives are interpreted through research I undertook over a ten-year period in Australian secondary schools. I recognize the difficulties and contradictions involved with this aim. First, with regard to its potential essentialism, and second, in relation to the much explored dilemmas that researchers face in imagining that subjects constructed out of their own research discourses are somehow independent of these discourses. These issues will be discussed in subsequent chapters.

## Difference pronounced deficit

In 1974, the Australian Schools Commission set the terms of reference for an inquiry into the educational needs of women and girls. This was in keeping with the spirit of reform initiated by the newly elected Labor government of the time and its emphasis on education as a vehicle for this reform. It was this government which established the Schools Commission, which in turn initiated the investigation to comment on the extent of female underachievement in education and the relationship between this and their inferior social status. It wanted some comment as to the reasons for their underachievement with particular reference to community attitudes and sex-based discrimination within schools. Of interest also was increased female participation in the labour force and its relationship to schooling. The

Schools Commission wanted the inquiry to 'recommend any program projects and the necessary funding to assist girls so that they have as many careers and life choices open to them as do boys' (Schools Commission 1975a: 1–2). The outcome of this inquiry was published in 1975 in the report *Girls, School and Society*.

*Girls, Schools and Society* (Schools Commission 1975a) has been very influential in shaping gender reform in Australian schools. The issues deemed important, the analysis offered, subsequent policy and interventionist programmes, can be traced to this foundational report (Yates 1987; Tsolidis 1993a). The understandings of ethnic minority girls embedded in this report arguably remained unchanged until 1987. This will be detailed in subsequent discussion.

The position adopted in *Girls, School and Society* illustrated a shift away from deficit models towards those associated with an inclusive curriculum. Assumptions about sex-based differences in learning styles were challenged. Instead, both girls and boys were judged capable of scientific, emotional and moral judgements. It was argued that schooling should value those skills traditionally associated with girls, such as intuition, creativity and interpersonal relationships, not only because this valuing provided girls with affirmation, but also because these skills were important in themselves (Schools Commission 1975a: 70). In this way, within the report, attention was drawn to the fact that so-called female skills were considered 'soft' in educational terms and were not valued because they 'cannot be cashed in higher education or jobs' (Schools Commission 1975a: 71). Highlighted within this report was the importance of schooling in assisting all students to take charge of their destinies. In conclusion the point was made that 'if girls see themselves as people for whom active conscious decision is not possible, that is the most damaging aspect of the process through which they have learned to be female' (Schools Commission 1975a: 111). It was argued that, at least initially, schools urgently needed to assist girls to change their view of themselves and construct a new reality in which their capacity to affect their circumstances and take conscious decisions was seriously taken.

Described within the report was how society limited girls' opportunities and self-perceptions and how schooling had a clear role and responsibility to rectify this situation by creating students who were themselves change-agents. It was argued that it was not a case of girls lacking skills, but of schooling not formally recognizing or rewarding the skills that they possessed, and as a consequence diminishing their self-perceptions. An important part of the change process identified was the need to alter these self-perceptions. *Girls, School and Society* represented a significant change of direction away from compensatory models which stressed the importance of pluralism at the expense of equity, to one which emphasized the culture of girls, a group of students who were understood to experience discrimination within the education system. Within such a framework, the position adopted in relation to ethnic minority girls is extremely pertinent.

Included in *Girls, School and Society* was a short chapter, peripheral to its overall argument, which addressed the needs of 'special' groups of girls. In this section were included 'migrant' girls, Aboriginal girls and girls from country regions. A total of 6 pages of the report, which was 194 pages in length, were devoted to 'migrant women and girls'; none of the conclusions or recommendations referred to this group specifically. Moreover, the 'migrants' referred to in *Girls, School and Society* were those from Greece, Italy and Yugoslavia only because they were 'the major groups in recent migration from non-English speaking countries' (Schools Commission 1975a: 135).

In the context of the discussion undertaken in Chapter 2, it is worthwhile to consider why a committee concerned with sexism and education would show so much interest in Greeks, Italians and Yugoslavs. These groups, rather than British or northern European immigrants, were discussed with reference to the special needs of 'migrant' girls. It has been argued that factors which make southern Europeans so distinguishable from mainstream Australians include physical appearance, their persistence in maintaining their mother-cultures and tongues, the visibility of their communities and their attitudes to family, particularly those pertaining to gender roles (Price 1963). In this context, it is easier to understand why, rather than an interest in immigrants *per se*, there was a concern in *Girls, School and Society* to discuss these three southern European communities. It is commonly understood that within these communities there exist different cultural norms pertaining to gender, relative to those within the Australian mainstream. Furthermore, this is understood to impact negatively on the educational participation of girls from these communities.

The committee responsible for the report was interested to investigate whether aspirations and performance were the same for girls and boys within these communities. Additionally, it wanted to investigate 'whether girls were particularly affected by cultural differences between home and school, and if so, how' (Schools Commission 1975a: 135). In summary, it was concluded that there were no indications that southern European girls performed less well than the boys from these communities. However, on the basis of 1971 figures, these girls were less likely to be at school at the ages of 16 and 18 than either mainstream Australian girls or boys from their communities. It was also concluded that although southern European families had generally higher educational aspirations than mainstream Australians from the same socio-economic background, these aspirations did not extend to their daughters. The conclusion about these parents' lower aspirations for their daughters was drawn, in part, on the basis of a then incomplete study conducted in Sydney by Martin and Meade (1979). This study tested students whose mothers came from southern European countries and found them to be below average on a range of verbal, numerical and non-verbal reasoning tests. However, because there existed no differences between the girls and boys in the southern European sample this was taken to indicate 'that culturally influenced sex role stereotypes are powerful in creating differential expectations' (Schools Commission 1975a: 138).

While, in an overall sense, attention was drawn to sexism and the influence it had on girls' aspirations, educational participation and achievement, in relation to southern European girls, their poor educational participation rates were explained in terms of cultural norms within their communities. Presumably, the overall sexism described in *Girls, School and Society* was not enough to explain the even lower participation rates by Greek, Italian and Yugoslav girls. Also, the fact that southern European boys did well, and in some instances, better than other boys, was taken to highlight the differential treatment between girls and boys within these communities. In this way, racism and its relationship to sexism, and the impact of this on the schooling experience of ethnic minority girls, were bypassed in the analysis presented in the report.

In relation to southern European girls, the committee responsible for *Girls, School and Society* used gender as its primary tool of analysis. Because of this, it could explain any existing differences between these and other girls, and between these girls and the boys within their communities, only in terms of exacerbated sexism within these communities. Moreover, the exacerbated sexism was explained in culturalist terms, as something intrinsic to these cultures, rather than a product of economic circumstances or the migration process, for example. An exception to this was the way that the issue of school-aged girls being withdrawn from school to do domestic duties for their parents was understood. It was argued that while all parents were more likely to keep daughters rather than sons home for such reasons, the likelihood of this being necessary was exaggerated within recently arrived immigrant families where both parents worked. In overall terms, however, in relation to southern European girls, the analysis provided failed to reflect factors such as racism, social dislocation or economic hardship or other by-products of the migration process.

Had the analysis contained in *Girls, School and Society* been initiated on a different premise, one which investigated the articulation between racism and sexism, the questions asked could have been very different. For example, if southern European girls had lower educational participation rates than the boys in their communities and girls in general, was the answer to be found in exacerbated sexism within their communities, or in an element of racism exacerbating the discrimination felt by girls in general? Did girls within these communities choose to leave school early because racism and sexism combined to make their schooling experience exceptionally alienating? Did they find the curriculum relevant and appropriate? Was the tendency for all girls to receive less schooling than boys exacerbated in these communities because of the additional hardships associated with the migration experience? The quality of the schooling experienced by southern European girls was not considered in the report. The relevance of the curriculum, language issues, school environment, methods of teaching, assessment, sense of achievement, peer-group interaction, role-models, experiences of overt racism and sexism – these were all issues which could have contributed to an explanation of why southern European girls may not have wanted to continue their education in Australian schools.

The failure within the report to consider such issues in relation to the educational experiences of southern European girls was particularly glaring given its overall focus on these very same issues with regard to girls in general. A significant element in the omission of such considerations by the committee was the view that it expressed of these students. They were not considered to be active agents who may have exercised a choice in the continuation of their schooling. Nowhere was a question framed which explored the possibility of these students choosing to leave school early because the experience was meaningless or unpleasant. Again, this analysis stands in strong contrast to the argument about girls in general, exemplified by the statement that 'if girls see themselves as people for whom active conscious decision is not possible, that is the most damaging aspect of the process through which they have learned to be female' (Schools Commission 1975a: 111).

While racism in relation to ethnic minority girls was ignored in the report, this was not the case in relation to Aboriginal girls. With reference to this group, gender was examined in relation to a range of contextualizing issues, including racism, the stress which assimilation placed on women, the need for solidarity between women and men who faced racism and also the need for oppressed groups to determine their own issues of concern. These arguments have clear corollaries with regard to ethnic minority communities and the girls within them, notwithstanding these remained unexplored in *Girls, School and Society*.

In a similar fashion there was a failure to consider class in relation to ethnicity. It was argued that the daughters of semi-skilled and unskilled workers were the most educationally disadvantaged, that family income affected girls' ability to enter the final year of secondary schooling more than boys, and that girls were also more strongly affected by their mothers' educational level. Potentially, these were important factors in explaining the lower educational participation rates of Greek, Italian and Yugoslav girls. Women from these communities were less educated, more likely to be in the workforce and if so, occupying lower skill occupations such as process work. While this was acknowledged within the report, no connections were made between this reality and the possible effect of it on their daughters' education.

*Girls, School and Society* is discussed in detail because it is one of the few and earliest examples of ethnic minority girls being addressed specifically within policy. However, the outcome of this has not been positive. Through the report were reinforced commonsense understandings of the ways in which gender relations operate within southern European communities. Moreover, a link was made between these relations and the educational experiences of girls from these communities. In summary, within the report, ethnic minority girls were considered within a deficit framework, whereby their agency was denied. Their subordination was constructed in culturalist terms and there was next to no mention of racism in relation to these girls or their communities. Arguably, the very nomination of these communities as worthy of special consideration, coincides with social-Darwinist under-standings of hierarchies of civilization and the feminist analysis of the importance of gender roles in the establishment of these, as discussed in Chapter 2.

## The invisibility of difference

Subsequent to *Girls, Schools and Society*, the Commonwealth Schools Com-mission published the report *Girls and Tomorrow: The Challenge for Schools*. This report (published in 1984) was the responsibility of the Work-ing Party on the Education of Girls, which was established in 1981 to give advice to the Commonwealth Schools Commission on related issues. This working party convened a national seminar on girls' education in 1982 and *Girls and Tomorrow* drew on this seminar for some of its material. The con-ference was convened around the four major themes of schooling process and structures; curriculum; science, mathematics and technology; and impli-cations of schooling for employment. As a consequence these issues were also the focus of the report. The reasons why these particular issues were given priority were never made explicit.

Unlike *Girls, School and Society*, the report *Girls and Tomorrow* did not break new ground. In many ways it simply reiterated the arguments made in the preceding report. The 1984 report placed an emphasis on implementing change. The working party responsible for it argued that the need for such change was established within the 1975 report and almost a decade later had yet to be enacted. However, the beguilingly simple strategies that were offered in *Girls and Tomorrow* did not reflect a depth of analysis commen-surate with that presented in *Girls, School and Society*. For example, in the recommendation related to curriculum, it was stated that 'curriculum con-tent at all levels of schooling be transformed in a way which provides for all students to acquire the competence and confidence to participate fully as independent and autonomous individuals in the social and economic life of the nation' (Commonwealth Schools Commission 1984: 11). In order for this to happen, it was recommended that materials and approaches be developed which could assist girls in mathematics, science and computers and which raised their self-esteem and acknowledged women's life experiences. One of the reasons the working party was able to make such uncomplicated recommendations was the fact that 'girls' were referred to as though they were a uniform category. In this way, differences between girls were avoided. With the exception of a statement outlining the need for research into 'the needs of girls facing specific disadvantages related to class or cultural background' (Commonwealth Schools Commission 1984: 20) there was no differentiation made in the report between groups of girls. Even this perfunctory statement evidenced an underpinning understanding that class and cultural difference were disadvantageous in themselves.

Within *Girls and Tomorrow* there was a review of developments in the area since the publication of *Girls, School and Society* and an agenda for change was established. This had as its core the development of a national policy dealing with girls' education. It was argued that Commonwealth Schools Commission grants, made on the basis of submissions, had created little change. Policy was seen as a means of transforming 'rhetoric into reality' (Commonwealth Schools Commission 1984: 9). This was so much so, that within the report one of six short chapters was dedicated to this issue and detailed a method for its implementation. In this way this report was noteworthy, not so much because of the analysis it offered on the issue, but because of the strategies it advocated for change, particularly the policy process it set in train.

### Difference and the politics of consultation

On the basis of *Girls and Tomorrow*, the Commonwealth Schools Commission initiated an intersystemic programme whereby a national policy on girls' education would be adopted. In 1986 the interim report *The Education of Girls in Australian Schools* was published (Commonwealth Schools Commission 1986). This became the basis for a lengthy consultation process. As a result of this consultation process, the first intersystemic, national policy of any kind was adopted. The following year *The National Policy for the Education of Girls in Australian Schools* was published (Commonwealth Schools Commission 1987). This policy provided a structure for system accountability. The analytical frameworks established in *Girls, School and Society* were adopted in the 1987 policy; however, the emphasis in the National Policy was placed on operationalizing a change process through policy at both school and system levels. A framework for action was established which was premised on a range of principles, objectives and priorities. Within this policy there were some shifts in emphasis, relative to other policy literature published. However, I would argue that these shifts were a product of the political nature of the consultation process rather than such shifts reflecting any changes in the theoretical conceptualization of the issues (Tsolidis 1993a).

The consultation process involved the Commonwealth government, States and territories, various education systems and communities. The significance of this process is most evident in relation to Aboriginal and Torres Strait Islander peoples. The emphasis on consultation provided these communities with the opportunity to contribute on their own terms and through their own community structures. As a result, girls' education in relation to these communities was discussed in a separate section of the National Policy and framed by the importance of issues related to land rights and self-determination.

This consultation process made an important difference to the vision of Aboriginality embedded in the policy and likewise produced a different emphasis in relation to ethnic minority girls. As I have argued elsewhere, lobby groups concerned with the representation of ethnic minority communities, particularly in relation to gender relations, were able to influence the framing of these issues within the National Policy (Tsolidis 1993a). As a result, unlike previous reports, ethnic minority girls' experiences of schooling were framed in relation to the migration process and systemic racism. There is clear reference in the National Policy to the benefits of cultural difference with the statement that schools have a 'cultural role in supporting girls from minority groups to develop a positive self-image by ensuring that cultural and related language differences are not turned into educational disadvantages or liabilities' (Commonwealth Schools Commission 1987: 9). In this way, there was a challenge to the deficit framing of cultural difference, which had been expounded in previous policy literature related to gender equity.

In 1993 the *National Action Plan for the Education of Girls 1993–1997* was published (Australian Education Council 1993). This was framed in relation to the National Policy and was intended to provide practical support for this policy. Within the Action Plan, eight priority areas were established as critical for schools to address. These included reforming the curriculum, changing school organization and management practice, improving teaching practice and examining the construction of gender. Each of these priority areas was presented with a rationale, strategies for implementation and system-level indicators.

More so than the other literature discussed here, the Action Plan illustrated shifts in feminist thinking which had occurred since the publication of *Girls, School and Society*. The Action Plan emphasized the constructedness of gender and the role of schooling in this process in relation to both femininity and masculinity. The role of context, language, beliefs and practices in creating different understandings of gender was outlined. In doing so, the Action Plan went some way towards a deconstructive approach, which acknowledged the ways in which polarities such as femininity and masculinity rely on each other for meaning. It also intimated the need for a progressive politics to challenge fixity of meaning by working through, rather than consolidating such dichotomies.

However, the Action Plan, like the National Policy, failed to incorporate notions of cultural difference in its overall analysis. There was inadequate consideration of how gender and cultural identifications articulate. Similarly, there was inadequate consideration of how all identifications are cultured, just as they are gendered. Instead, cultural difference was understood to apply simply to ethnic minority girls. Within such policy existed an understanding of gender, which acknowledged the need to challenge dichotomies. However, there was no equivalent understanding of how concepts such as ethnic minority and ethnic majority rely on each other for meaning and how the latter term is privileged in educational discourses, including those related to gender equity.

Within these gender equity policies can be traced various understandings of cultural difference. There are examples of the invisibility of difference, difference as deficit and a political intervention instigated by the 'different' during a process of consultation; the latter, with all the ensuing contradictions of speaking from the margins and the propensity of this to reinscribe the centrality of the existing centre. Notions of invisibility, difference as deficit and interventions based on cultural difference and their political implications have all been debated and theorized within feminist discourses, particularly those related to racism. These will be discussed in more detail in subsequent chapters. It is not difficult to articulate a position on the basis of such policy, that within discourses centred on the notion of equity, difference can become subsumed and that anti-hegemonic interventions can create in themselves consolidations of various other hegemonies. In the next section I wish to consider education policies concerned with multiculturalism. As in the case of gender equity policy, the primary concern here is to consider the ways in which ethnic minority girls are represented within such multicultural policies. Do differences exist between these policies *vis-à-vis* gender? Are representations of ethnic minority girls within them different from those that exist within the gender equity policies already discussed?

## Ethnicity and education: equity or pluralism?

The period of optimism surrounding the reform potential of education which produced *Girls, School and Society* found that the Schools Commission also produced statements on what should constitute a relevant education with regard to cultural difference. As with gender, the Schools Commission was concerned to frame this around notions of inequality linked to socio-economic status (Tsolidis 1993a). Its first Triennium Report (1975b) provided a comprehensive statement on what constituted appropriate multicultural education.

Within this report, the Schools Commission extended what had hitherto been known as 'migrant education' beyond the teaching of English to non-English speakers. It highlighted the need for mother-tongue and cultural maintenance and recognized the important role that these played for students' self-esteem and learning. It recognized the need for a two-way process, which required the education of both the mainstream and the minorities. It also challenged the understandings which had dominated previous English as Second Language programmes. Rather than specialist staff withdrawing minority students into separate programmes and separate rooms to learn English, there were references to bilingual programmes, professional development programmes for non-specialist staff so that they could take some responsibility for these students' acquisition of English, and the provision of resources so that specialist and non-specialist staff could work together on the development of language-appropriate curriculum. In these ways the education of ethnic minority students had the potential to become integrated into the mainstream life of a school, rather than remain peripheral.

In 1977 the Australian Commonwealth Government appointed a committee to review services available to ethnic minority communities. The committee (with Frank Galbally as its chairman) produced the report entitled *Review of Post Arrival Programs and Services to Migrants*, which is more commonly referred to as the Galbally Report (Committee of Review of Post Arrival Programs and Services for Migrants 1978). In relation to education, this review advocated the establishment of the Multicultural Education Program and through it allocated A$5 million specifically to assist with the development of multicultural curriculum. The rights of ethnic minorities to maintain their cultural identity and the need for all students to acquire knowledge of Australia's multicultural character were advocated. The allocation of A$5 million was intended to stimulate a range of initiatives including the teaching of community languages and cultures, bilingual approaches, multicultural perspectives programmes, related teacher professional development, relevant materials development, parent and community involvement and research.

The Review Committee responsible for the Galbally Report drafted its recommendations under broad guiding principles. These stressed equal opportunity and access, cultural maintenance and tolerance, the need for specialist services and programmes as an interim measure towards the issues being taken up by existing programmes, and the importance of self-help towards self-reliance. The understanding of multiculturalism that underpinned the report equated pluralism with democracy and social cohesion. It was argued:

> Provided that ethnic identity is not stressed at the expense of society at large, but is interwoven into the fabric of our nationhood by the process

of multicultural interaction, then the community as a whole will benefit substantially and its democratic nature will be reinforced.

(Committee of Review of Post Arrival Programs and Services for
Migrants 1978: 104)

Within this framework, respect for cultural difference was expected to guarantee social cohesion by fostering in ethnic minorities a sense of security. However, questions of cultural identity and social cohesion were treated as though they stood separately from factors such as class or gender.

The positions adopted in the Galbally Report and the first Triennium Report of the Schools Commission represented quite divergent approaches to equity and difference. The Schools Commission attempted to address difference within a framework, which in an overall sense was concerned with equity. However, as Jakubowicz *et al.* (1984) argued, through the Galbally Report, there was presented a separation of the cultural and the economic, the latter erased from the analysis thereby sustaining: 'class relations by concentration on the cultural, interpersonal and communications manifestations of those relations. So too, the role of migrant women was totally left out of the analysis – except for a token and ritualistic nod in their direction' (Jakubowicz *et al.* 1984: 78).

### Defining multicultural education

In order to furnish guidelines for the distribution of this A$5 million, two Commonwealth Committees were established. In its report *Education for a Multicultural Society*, the Committee on Multicultural Education (1979: 10) stated a preference for the phrase 'education for a multicultural society' because it indicated a 'philosophy which permeates the total work of the school' rather than a strand of education which was implicit in the term 'multicultural education'. Similarly, it stressed that education for a multicultural society was intended for the whole community not just for schools with large percentages of ethnic minority students. Three areas of work were identified as particularly significant. These were relationships between schools and homes and students and teachers; the curriculum, particularly multicultural perspectives and language teaching and learning; and support mechanisms including training, research and communication of information (Committee on Multicultural Education 1979: 11).

*Education for a Multicultural Society* included a series of recommendations on how schools should approach multiculturalism. The relationship between the home and the school was emphasized within these. The possibility of conflict between the cultures of the home and those of the school was highlighted. Different constructions of gender within the home and the school were emphasized as a potential source of this conflict. The committee offered a range of strategies to assist schools communicate with ethnic minority homes.

The second committee, the Commonwealth Education Portfolio Group, produced a discussion paper entitled *Education in a Multicultural Australia*, also published in 1979. The aim was to clarify the term 'multicultural education' because the Portfolio Group considered that no consensus existed around the concept, but instead was concerned that it 'may divide the community by highlighting existing differences rather than foster understanding, tolerance and social cohesion' (Commonwealth Education Portfolio Group 1979: 1). In line with the Galbally Report, the Portfolio Group stressed cohesion through diversity. It identified several elements within Australian society, which protected this cohesion. These were national institutions such as parliament and the legal system, English as the lingua franca, and shared values, primarily those of democracy and egalitarianism. The last page of the discussion paper addressed equality and drew attention to the tension between it and difference specifically. In order to illustrate this tension it referred to 'the traditional role for women held by some ethnic groups and equality of the sexes espoused by the school system' (Commonwealth Education Portfolio Group 1979: 23).

In this way, the Portfolio Group's discussion paper, like the other report, did not address gender specifically. The role that gender played in creating inclusionary/exclusionary boundaries was implied through reference to home–school communication and the relationship between equity and difference respectively. This had the status of commonsense knowledge rather than an issue, which warranted exploration and elaboration in its own right. In relation to the place of ethnic minority girls in these policy documents, what remains significant is either their invisibility or the construction of them as exemplars of 'culture clash' and its potential threat to Australian social cohesion.

It is important to note that the multicultural policies described here are early ones and that a significant challenge was posed to the position adopted within these in subsequent policies. In the 1980s, a shift in emphasis occurred and attempts were made to integrate equity and difference. Within these subsequent policies there was explicit consideration of gender and class. These policies will be considered further in subsequent chapters.

It is significant that both within policy dealing with gender, which I have argued represents a concern with equity, and policy dealing with multiculturalism with its emphasis on difference, the construction of ethnic minority girls remains the same. These students remain invisible, are conceptualized in deficit terms and seen as victims of 'culture clash'. In both sets of policy, the dominant view is one that considers these girls to be in a worse situation to that of other girls and boys from their communities. Further to this, this situation is understood to be a product of their communities and culturally determined perspectives within these related to gender relations.

Perhaps one difference between these two sets of policies is that within those concerned with multiculturalism these girls are used to illustrate the potential dilemmas for democratic societies aiming at both equity and respect of difference. Those policies concerned with gender equity express a concern for the girls themselves. As a means of bringing this exploration of policy to a close, I would like to consider a specific policy debate of particular significance for its potential to indicate some ways forward.

### Challenging the home versus school binary

In *Girls, Schools and Society* attention was drawn to the importance of sex education for girls. The sexual double standard and the role that this played in the lowering of girls' self-esteem and the disincentive it provided for independent thought and decision-making by girls was described. The teaching of sex education within schools was advocated and the statement made that this be done 'within the context of human relationships and of sex roles and in a non-prescriptive manner' (Schools Commission 1975a: 121). The report of the Victorian Committee on Equal Opportunity in Schools (1977) also took up the link between sexuality and women's inferior role within society. It suggested that schools had a responsibility to teach about sex and human relations and that this would have 'the effect of increasing girls' self-esteem and the dignity and esteem in which women are held' (Victorian Committee on Equal Opportunity in Schools 1977: 154). The committee believed that this would lead to a more equitable and open view of women and men in domestic and work roles.

In 1979 the Victorian government established the Advisory Committee on Health and Human Relations Education in Schools to provide guidelines on this matter. Yates (1987b) argues that the very title, 'Health and Human Relations', pointed to the controversy surrounding the issue and functioned as a euphemism for two of its components – sex and values education. She contended that in part the controversy associated with this issue related to the encroachment of school into an area traditionally considered the responsibility of the family. The Concerned Parents Association campaigned against the introduction of Health and Human Relations courses and the final government disassociation with the issue was made on the basis of the separation of scholarship, considered a function of schooling, and issues associated with sex and morality considered not to be so (Yates 1987b).

In recognition of this tension between the role of schooling and that of the family, advocates of sex education stressed the importance of the family and the community within such courses. The role of parents was underscored within the report issued by the Consultative Council for Health and Human Relations Education. Chapter 3 of the report was headed 'The role of parents and the community' and began with the statement 'Parents are the

Primary Educators in Health and Human Relations' (Consultative Council for Health and Human Relations Education 1980: 8). The report emphasized the central role that parents had in the determination of values and the need for cooperation between home and school in such matters. Consultation, it was suggested, was more than informing parents about what needed to be taught, but was an exchange of ideas, negotiation when differences arose, trust developed through face-to-face contact between parents and teachers, and the provision by schools of pertinent information.

While debates surrounding the teaching of health and human relations in Victoria (in the 1980s) may seem somewhat obscure in relation to the deliberations being undertaken here, they are in some respects central. One of the arguments being framed is that home–school relations have been constructed as critical within education debates related to equity and difference. In such frameworks, the home has come to represent specificity, juxtaposed to the school, most often seen to represent a means of inducting minority students into the mainstream and the bodies of knowledge which are socially enabling. Through the debate about the teaching of sex education, we are presented with an example of progressive educators attempting to change the nature of the bodies of knowledge all students need to access. This debate occurred at a time when the dominant discourses relating to gender equity (as has been discussed), either through omission or explicit statement, were complicit in the representation of cultural difference as problematic. This being particularly so with regard to southern European communities and presumptions that within these communities, gender relations reinforced rather than challenged the feminist policy agenda and the teaching of sex education it advocated. In this context, how progressive educators understood home–school relations becomes a critical indication of how they addressed the tension between equity and difference with particular relevance to gender equity and cultural diversity. Quite distinct perspectives were manifest in the various reports on this issue.

Within *Girls, School and Society* the need for cooperation between the home and school and the valuable role that parents had in such programmes, both as co-decision-makers and resource people, was argued. However, it was explicitly stated that should conflict arise between the family and the school on such matters, the school should not refrain from teaching sex education and human relations, but should seek the assistance of counsellors who could mediate (Schools Commission 1975a: 122). In this way, it was an argument that respect for cultural difference should not take precedence over the implementation of the reforms in question. If conflict arose between the school and the ethnic minority family, the school should seek the assistance of counsellors, preferably ones familiar with the ethnic minority culture in question, to mediate. There was no question of the school modifying its goal or developing a curriculum in line with the community's expectations. This position contrasted to the one adopted by the

Victorian Committee on Equal Opportunity in Schools (1977: 157), which stressed that school-based curriculum development in the area should 'not cut across the moral beliefs and philosophies held by the families from which the students come'. In broad terms, these positions can be seen to represent, in the case of the former, difference being relevant only in terms of the means by which the same ends are achieved, and in the case of the latter, pluralism overriding equity concerns, in the context of understanding sex education as a gender equity reform.

In contrast to both these positions, the report issued by the Consultative Council for Health and Human Relations Education (1980) stressed the importance of home–school communication in a process whereby teachers and parents learnt about each other's positions, negotiated and compromised as a means of resolving the tension between equity and difference in such situations. It was written within a framework which accounted for cultural difference and moreover, the power differential linked to it. It argued that some families had an 'anxiety about the dominant Anglo-Australian culture' (Consultative Council for Health and Human Relations Education 1980: 11) and that all teachers, particularly those teaching health and human relations, needed to be sensitive towards cultural difference and its impact on curriculum planning and implementation. Through this report the onus was placed on the school to become familiar with what ethnic minority communities would wish for their children. The Consultative Council responsible for it suggested practical strategies to enhance communication and trust between families and schools. In order to achieve this, the Council advocated the use of bilingual and bicultural staff, the need for all teachers to be aware of and respect cultural diversity, the need for teachers to learn about minority cultures, the translation of relevant materials into home languages and the use of established ethnic minority networks to facilitate communication. Rather than stress the use of mediators who could familiarize the parents with what the school was doing, the emphasis in this report was on how the school could better inform itself on issues related to these communities. The position outlined in this report represented a more equitable power distribution between home and school. Moreover, it assumed a dynamic relationship between communities and schools and the possibility this created for two-way communication, compromise and change.

Between these three positions were represented two opposing understandings of culture. This is a difference that is fundamental to the debate about difference and equity. Both the position adopted in *Girls, School and Society* and the report by the Victorian Committee on Equal Opportunity in Schools (1977), I would argue, are premised on the same view of culture. Culture is constructed as a static and irrevocably bounded phenomenon. There is the culture of the mainstream, mediated through the school, and the cultures of the minorities, mediated through the home. Because of the understanding of culture as static, we are left with little option but to take sides. Moreover, this construction of culture plays into an established political schema whereby equity, defined as sameness, coincides with the mainstream; difference, as its opposite, coincides with a reactionary pluralism. This is particularly evident in the example discussed here. *Girls, School and Society* is strongly identified with a period in Australian history which saw the ascendancy of the Labor Party and through it a renewed interest in social justice and the role of education within such a reform agenda. On the other hand, the Victorian policy was framed by a context where conservative politics emphasized choice and the individual.

Such an understanding of culture as static and bounded means that the role that schooling can play is also limited to a choice between supporting the mainstream (equity) or supporting minorities (difference). Again this is evident in the two reports discussed here. The committee responsible for *Girls, School and Society* is surefooted in its response to this situation. If attempts to bring the home into line with the mainstream fail, there is no doubt about the responsibility of the school to implement the policy agenda. Similarly, the Victorian policy is surefooted in the opposite direction.

The report from the Consultative Council for Health and Human Relations Education (1980), on the other hand, adopts an alternative view of culture. Culture is fluid and there is potential for contestation, negotiation and reinterpretation. Culture is not irrevocably bounded by relations as these operate either within the mainstream or minority communities but instead is framed by the specificity of the particular context and moment. In this framework, the school represents a means of facilitating new cultural understandings because it provides the space between the mainstream and the minorities. The relatively democratic, two-way process advocated is in line with a politics of difference with the potential of defining equity as something other than sameness.

While the above review of relevant literature issued by national and Victorian educational authorities is intended to explore the construction of ethnic minority girls, the overwhelming conclusion relates more to their invisibility. They were not referred to in a way which constituted them as active subjects. Instead, the issue of home–school communication was highlighted and gender relations were used to exemplify the possible conflict, which can arise between the values of the school and the ethnic minority family. Various viewpoints were expressed in relation to this conflict and the means for its resolution, but in relation to ethnic minority girls, one is left to interpret silences and invisibility. This was the case even in relation to *Girls, School and Society*, where although they were referred to specifically, the framework in which this was done did not constitute them as subjects. Instead, the overwhelming impression from the policy documents is one of others, not sharing their experiences or perspectives, looking in on them from the outside and of their voice not being heard. It would seem that the only difference between *Girls, School and Society* and the other literature was that the former articulated a construction of ethnic minority women and girls the others assumed; that is, a negative construction of them as objects, as silent, as victims caught in a culture clash.

The culture clash model has commonly been used to provide a framework in discussions related to ethnicity and schooling. It is of particular significance because it assumes the important role played by gender in the creation of boundaries between ethnicities. In it, gender is seen to highlight the difference between 'them and us'. Although there were differences within the literature regarding the solution to this culture clash which corresponded, in some ways, to the position adopted *vis-à-vis* the equity/difference dilemma, the clash itself and its link to gender was not disputed.

While gender was seen as instrumental in creating boundaries between 'them and us', what constituted the various constructions of gender remained assumed rather than explored. From the various reports can be gleaned an understanding of gender as it is constructed in southern European cultures relative to the Australian mainstream, created more on the basis of commonsense knowledge than any serious investigation, and certainly an understanding which was developed without the involvement of ethnic minority communities. The exception to this is *The National Policy on the Education of Girls in Australian Schools* (Commonwealth Schools Commission 1987) where a fundamentally political process of consultation allowed particular lobby groups, concerned with cultural difference, to have some influence on the shaping of the issues as these related to ethnic minority girls (Tsolidis 1993b). Because of this, racism and the process of migration are referred to, as are the potentially positive aspects of cultural difference and the role of schooling in supporting minority identifications. More generally, however, multicultural and gender equity policy espouses the notion that the oppression experienced by minority girls is primarily caused by the enactment of gender relations within their communities. Further to this, mainstream society, represented through the school, has the potential to offer them some form of emancipation from these gender relations.

As discussed in Chapter 2, understandings of gender relations within minority communities have functioned as an indicator for their potential to assimilate into mainstream Australian society. Moreover, these have been judged within hierarchical understandings of culture as more or less civilized. It is for these reasons that culture clash models have been perceived as particularly salient in relation to ethnic minority girls, particularly those from southern Europe. These communities have been traditionally considered less desirable because of perceived differences between them and the mainstream, and gender relations have been one criterion on which this judgement has been made. It is in this context that adolescent girls from such communities become targets in expressions of assimilation which have at their heart an understanding of gender relations within these communities as particularly patriarchal. Such understandings are embedded in a range of discourses including education policy discourses concerned with gender equity and multiculturalism.

In relation to such discourses, the views about the hierarchies of culture and the significance of gender relations in demarking these has been argued most often with regard to ethnic minority girls and educational aspirations and their ability to socialize in manners common within mainstream Australian society. On both of these issues, the assumption has been that expressions of patriarchy within such communities explain disadvantages that these girls experience, more so than other factors, including racism within Australian society.

Within most of the relevant policy literature, particularly that dated between 1975 and 1984, the dominant framework used to position ethnic minority girls related to the culture clash model. Accepted within multicultural and gender equity policy, from various perspectives and for various reasons, was the notion that students from minority cultures, particularly southern European ones, faced a distinct set of values, traditions and lifestyles which stood in stark contradiction to those of mainstream Australian society, represented through schooling. This understanding was considered particularly relevant during adolescence and in relation to girls. The culture clash model warrants some exploration because of its prevalence within policy literature and because of its currency within commonsense understandings of these students' situations.

The culture clash model assumes a vision of culture as static with the intention of keeping minority difference quarantined from the mainstream. In relation to youth, it is the intent to assist them to become 'Australian' for philanthropic reasons or for reasons related to the common good of social cohesion, which is assumed to require assimilation. In line with this view is the consideration that for young people, especially girls, this swapping of cultural locations is a privilege recognized as an outcome of their parents' immigration, which they want or need. These issues are encapsulated by a teacher's comment that 'The best thing you can do for NESB [non-English-speaking background] girls is get them to marry ESB [English-speaking background] boys' (Tsolidis 1986). Through this comment, we are presented with yet another example of the perception of difference as threat, the lack of agency attributed to such girls, the assumed superiority of the mainstream and the role of gender and sexuality *vis-à-vis* ethnicity. The vision of culture embedded in culture clash analyses is extremely problematic. Apart from the construction of difference as undesirable, an assumption is made that cultures are in fact static and that the power relations which are embedded within them result in delineated and immutable binaries between the minority and majority, 'them and us', Australian and other. Instead, the argument developed here is one which illustrates that culture is a dynamic concept and that gender relations are at the crux of processes which are developing new understandings of Australianness.

# 4    Going out or staying in: sexuality, schooling and assimilation

Imagine Inge, a 16-year-old Turkish Cypriot. Her father and mother left Cyprus after the 1974 Turkish invasion of Cyprus to start a new life in Australia. They opened a restaurant in a busy inner-city area of Melbourne and worked night and day to establish themselves and their family. Inge and her sister were studious but found bridging the gap between their Cypriot and Australian education difficult, especially given the long hours they worked helping their parents in the family restaurant. Moreover, Inge had a secret. Since leaving Cyprus she had been writing to her boyfriend, who was left behind. After two years she decided to tell her parents and a trip back home was made to arrange the details of the wedding.

Imagine Inge's teachers. The inner-city school that she attended prided itself on its progressive curriculum, a strong component of which was an equal opportunity programme for girls. The curriculum included, along with huge amounts of English as a Second Language (ESL), a unit in Herstory and girls-only outdoor education programmes and camps. In the context of the late 1970s and early 1980s this was heady stuff.

Imagine the reaction to Inge's wedding photographs and the fact that as a dowry the young couple had been presented with a new, completely furnished, brick house, part of the prestigious estate on the hill. This was in marked contrast to the small, most often timber, workers' cottages in which most students lived. The other students in the ESL class well understood and appreciated the white dress, good-looking groom and house. Many of the teachers, however, could hardly comprehend what seemed to them to be a young life nipped in the bud. They were dismayed and angered by traditions and value-systems which they understood as almost feudal and certainly exceptionally patriarchal; they preferred that this way of life stayed in the Cypriot village rather than be transported to Australia. The teachers, that is, who did not share a cultural background which made Inge's world seem familiar.

For the ESL teachers, who were Greek, Lebanese and Serbian and who were women trying to bridge the lives of their students and the wide world beyond the ESL portable classrooms clustered at the back of the school yard, overlooking the neighbouring steelworks, Inge's situation presented no black and white alternatives. Yes, in one way, it was a tragedy that Inge did not have the opportunity, at this stage of her life, to explore a fuller range of options. But she did have a relationship she had chosen to enter, the security of an extended family network, a career and financial stability in an increasingly insecure economic climate. (The year after her wedding Inge and her husband opened their own very successful restaurant.) Expressed in an alternative mind-set these same elements could combine into a fine set of progressive, even emancipatory, qualities – a young woman defying her parents to enter a love-match of her own choosing, self-sufficient and successful in a non-traditional career.

Within most of the educational discourses described in Chapter 3, ethnic minority girls remain invisible or are presented in ways that deny their agency. Most commonly, the issue of gender is used as an exemplar of the discordance between family and school values which schools must negotiate in a multicultural community. In this regard, policies related to ethnic difference do not differ from policies concerned more specifically with gender. At the school level, this discordance translates into a list of supposedly good things about Australian society, which are presumed not to exist in minority cultures. Consequently there are explorations of priorities and strategies relevant in getting the families to do what schools consider need to be done; getting Turkish girls to attend school camps, getting Greek boys to be less macho, getting ethnic minority parents to understand the value of sex education or camp programmes.

While multicultural approaches have challenged deficit notions of minority cultures, such policies have also been, most often, silent on the question of class and gender. Cultural difference is explored solely in relation to ethnicity as though this were a stand-alone issue. In this way, these policies avoid the hard questions related to the distribution of power, within frameworks which privilege pluralism.

A common outcome of the way that gender relations are understood to operate within minority cultures is the denial of agency to minority women. Most often, minority culture is constructed as if it were synonymous with the patriarchal thus denying the female and feminist traditions within minority cultures. Moreover, implicit in such constructions is an understanding of mainstream culture as relatively enlightened and able to offer ethnic minority women and girls a better deal than minority cultures.

On the whole, there has existed very little overlap between policies concerned with the education of girls and those concerned with ethnic status. On the contrary there persist strong commonsense understandings among Australian educationists that the two areas of gender and ethnicity are separate and incompatible. This sense of incompatibility can be attributed to racism implicit in hierarchies of oppression as these relate to cross-cultural understandings of gender relations (hooks 1981; Parmar 1982; hooks 1984; Mama 1984; Ramazanoglu 1989; Phoenix 1990; Huggins 1991; Pettman 1992; Ng 1995).

I would like to return to Inge to illustrate this point. For many, Inge's situation is symptomatic of a culturally specific form of patriarchy, which is worse than patriarchy as it is expressed in mainstream Australian society. Given this summation, it is an easy step to take to imagine that Inge would be better off assimilating into the Australian way of doing things which, on the face of it, would offer her, as a young woman, more opportunities than the Turkish-Cypriot way of doing things.

What is the basis of an understanding, which has constructed Inge as oppressed and her young ethnic majority classmates less so? Inge shared a classroom with the types of mainstream students whom many teachers, at the time, referred to affectionately as members of the duffle-coat and moccasin brigade. These were working-class girls who were not members of ethnic minority communities. They were mostly perceived as not particularly ambitious and not particularly interested in schooling. Often these young women were not experiencing much success at school, many were in exploitative sexual relationships and had their horizons restricted by poverty, early motherhood and limited educational success. None the less, there was a commonsense understanding that on some indices they were somehow better off than the likes of Inge. In part, this understanding was based on distinctions drawn between notions of individualistic free will relative to extended family obligations centred on notions of reputation and responsibility. In school-yard parlance, these distinctions translated into the difference between being street-wise or over-protected. And they were expressed clearly in relation to ethnic status.

In relation to Inge, her sense of obligation to her family to maintain an honourable reputation by marrying her boyfriend, and her family's responsibility to her in the form of a dowry, encumber any analysis which may stress her free will in entering the relationship, her judgement about her educational potential and her business acumen. However, in the case of the street-wise 16-year-old, it is her free will and ability to fulfil her desires that are stressed, rather than the social forces at work which make exploitative sexual relationships, for example, seem imperative (Thomas 1980). In the case of both girls, their agency functions within a context shaped by a vast range of factors including those related to ethnicity and class. This range of contextualizing factors will afford each girl advantages and disadvantages. Yet in the case of the street-wise 16-year-old, the emphasis is on her capacity to fulfil her desires and not on the restrictions which frame her agency in ways that may lead to further constraints on choice. For Inge, on the other hand, the emphasis is on the restrictions and not on her agency. Both types of girls benefit very little from attempts to generalize the factors which shape such contexts or in prioritizing some factors over others and furthermore, implying hierarchies of worth between them.

Policy discourses concerned with girls education and multiculturalism can fulfil a regulatory function in relation to ethnic minority girls because such discourses do not account for specificity of experience. Most specifically, regardless of the fact that policy concerned with girls and that concerned with ethnicity deal with equality and difference respectively, both deny ethnic minority women and girls' agency instead of recognizing that this agency functions within specifically constituted parameters. Without this recognition, such educational discourses may in fact fulfil a regulatory function, not only in relation to students like Inge, but also in relation to other groups of girls.

Inge is a student whom I taught when I worked as one of the ESL teachers referred to above. Her experiences, and the staff's response to them, constitute one element which has prompted and shaped my interest in the issues under consideration here. In this chapter, I would like to pursue issues that evolve out of Inge's experience, through a broader framework. This will be done through discussion of two research projects for which I was responsible, one beginning in 1984 and the other in 1994. Both of these projects were funded by government agencies concerned with multiculturalism and each had different purposes; importantly, each reflects different understandings of the issues of concern. Additionally, each reflects different understandings of how research is framed. None the less, they have much in common with each other and I am optimistic that on this basis, the differences between them will add an interesting dimension to the exploration of the questions under investigation. I shall discuss each study separately before going on to explore some of the implications of the various research approaches. Similarly, exploration of the insights, which can be drawn between these studies, will be undertaken in a subsequent chapter.

## Educating Voula

Historically, Victoria has been one of the most ethnically diverse states in Australia. Associated with manufacturing, it has attracted a large number of post-Second World War immigrants. Many issues associated with the crystallization of the ethnic rights movement have been played out in the Victorian context. The riots by immigrants at the Ford motor plant in 1973 have been considered critical to the development of minority activism. These riots were triggered by a sense of outrage at the employment conditions at the plant and the association of these with southern European 'factory fodder' (Lever-Tracy 1984).

Ethnic communities in Victoria have had a strong presence through key organizations such as the Australian Greek Welfare Society, which have been instrumental in shifting government funding to ethno-specific service provision. Additionally, minority communities have had strong representation through peak bodies, primarily the Victorian Ethnic Communities Council (Foster and Stockley 1988; Foster 1988). In this context, it is understandable that in the early 1980s a newly elected State Labor government would have a forthright agenda related to ethnic minority issues. Much as at the national level, the incoming Victorian Labor government ushered in a change agenda after decades of conservative rule. Similarly, education was a critical component and this was symbolized by the creation of the State Board of Education, on which there were representatives from parent associations, teacher unions and ethnic communities. The government position on education was expressed through six ministerial papers issued through this body (Minister of Education 1985). The then Minister for Education also changed the membership and structure of the Ministerial Advisory Committee on Multicultural and Migrant Education to include representatives from ethnic minority communities. This committee was charged with providing related advice and overseeing the dispersal of the funds recommended by the Galbally Report (Committee of Review of Post Arrival Programs and Services for Migrants 1978) for use in multicultural education. (This report will be further discussed subsequently.) It is significant that one of the first research projects initiated by this committee related to ethnic minority girls and education. This is the study referred to here that was conducted between 1984 and 1986. Its key findings were published as a government report entitled *Educating Voula: A Report on Non-English Speaking Background Girls and Education* (Tsolidis 1986).

The sponsoring committee for this study had clear aims and framed the study accordingly. This needs to be considered in the context of the discussion of policies undertaken previously. The committee intended that this study should address similar issues to those emphasized in *Girls, School and Society*, for example, ethnic minority girls' work and study aspirations. However, the committee sought an exploration of these issues which centred the viewpoint of ethnic minority girls. Additionally an emphasis was placed on factors which contextualized these issues, primarily class and migration. A clear incentive for the committee, in establishing the study, was to challenge the prevailing stereotypes surrounding the construction of gender within ethnic minority communities, by providing a context for the issues which had hitherto remained unexplored in policy literature issued by education authorities (Lo Bianco 1986).

Although the proposal was an attempt to establish what could broadly be described as an affirmative perspective on the educational experiences of ethnic minority girls, it was, none the less, predicated on a perceived need by members of Australia's ethnic minority communities to mount a defence of themselves in light of mainstream representations of gender relations within their communities. Arguably, the questions selected by the committee for inclusion in the study proposal were a response to the conclusions put forward in *Girls, School and Society* that ethnic minority communities had lower aspirations for their daughters than those they had for their sons and that in relation to sex-roles, especially pertaining to women and girls, their values were very distinct from those of the mainstream. It was suggested that the latter point was the cause of personal conflict for ethnic minority girls because they were presented with two distinct sets of values, one associated with the home and the other with the school. This view of ethnic minority communities is one which has dogged proponents of multiculturalism and to which the original proposal was a response. While it stressed the need for an affirmative perspective, which centred the experiences and reality of ethnic minority women and girls, the committee actually took as its starting point the view of these girls and their communities as it was represented in most policy literature already discussed. (More details related to this study are provided in Appendix 1.)

Mainly, this study was conducted at three schools, which were deemed by government definitions at the time to be socio-economically disadvantaged. I conducted the research by teaching at these schools over a two-year period. These schools enrolled predominantly ethnic minority students. My classes were made up of ethnic minority girls only. Through various subjects and curricula, students in these classes were given the opportunity to reflect on their lives, aspirations and schooling experiences. In some cases this work resulted in classroom materials which were subsequently produced by the Ministry for Education as a way of supplying students with materials which were inclusive of ethnic minority girls' interests and experiences (MACMME undated, 1986, 1987, 1988; Tsolidis 1989).

On the basis of this work, questionnaires and worksheets were developed and these became the basis for focus group discussions and activities with other groups of students. This work was short term and the intention was to maintain the centrality of the ethnic minority girls' perspective. The other students were divided into three single-sex categories consisting of ethnic majority girls and boys and ethnic minority boys. It was anticipated that this method would allow the interrelationship between gender and ethnicity to be explored through comparisons between ethnic minority girls and boys and ethnic minority girls and other girls.

The following discussion includes the views of the four groups of students, described in the original study as NESB (non-English-speaking background) girls and boys and ESB (English-speaking-background) girls and boys, the common bureaucratic nomenclature of the day, across all the schools involved. It is intended to develop issues of particular relevance to the arguments in this book, rather than provide an overview of the study itself. In some instances, there is more detailed exploration of particular groups of students to illustrate specific issues.

## Gender relations

> My mum lets him [brother] go out whenever he feels because she feels
> he can look after himself.
>
> (Roula, Year 10)

Similar to 16-year-old Roula, quoted above, male and female students from
both minority and mainstream ethnic groups felt that within their families,
more restrictions were placed on girls. Relative to their sons, their parents
did not allow daughters to go out as often, stay out as late and were more
concerned with whom the girls went out. However, in various contexts
students discussed restrictions, which were seen to operate on ethnic minority girls specifically.

These girls faced the sexual double-standard that all girls faced but had to
negotiate this through the added burden of socializing in a country where
their parents remained unfamiliar with and suspicious of the dominant
social mores. These difficulties were consolidated by the emphasis within
their communities on honour and reputation.

> Parents become afraid of gossip, the reason they fear gossip is once a
> girl gets a bad name, then the girl is labelled as promiscuous and ill-
> mannered. The reasons boys are more free is because the parents believe
> the boys can not be labelled or lose their reputation.
>
> (Fatima, Year 12)

Girls, through comparisons with lifestyles in their countries of origin,
described the detrimental impact of migration on the negotiation of the
double-standard. This was established on the basis of their lives prior to
migration, during trips back or through correspondence with friends and
relatives who had not migrated.

> In Turkey my cousins are more free than me because there are hardly
> any other nationalities living in Turkey like in Australia. So there, their
> parents don't have to worry much but over here I'm not free because my
> parents are scared something might happen to me. My father is think-
> ing of going back to Turkey forever in another one or two years' time
> so I am looking forward to going back to my home country.
>
> (Gemila, Year 12)

> My parents started not to let me out as much as they used to in Greece.
> I could not understand why at first, but then I realized myself that we
> were in a new country and we were surrounded by new people whom
> they did not know. I find that I belong in Greece. I like Melbourne
> but I find that the night life here is very boring. In Greece even sitting
> in a coffee shop entertains you because you know everyone, everyone

speaks the same language and people talk to you even if they have never seen you before. Here in Melbourne, I find that people are snobs.

(Penny, Year 12)

Boys from these communities were in a contradictory location, implicated in maintaining the honour of the family through their guardianship of their sisters and yet understanding the disjuncture of this within the context of Australian youth and school cultures. Additionally, they lived this contradiction in relation to their relatively privileged lifestyles. The boys echoed the comments made by girls within their communities about the restrictions they faced and the 'the old ladies making up and exaggerating things' and the rumours that were spread about them as a form of social control. The policing of these girls through the maintenance or otherwise of their reputations was freely acknowledged as an oppressive factor in these girls' lives.

These ethnic minority girls and boys described various means of addressing this policing and these varied from community to community, as well as within communities. Ethnic minority boys were implicated in this policing through the expectation that they accompany sisters or other female family members during outings when parents were not present. Boys responded to a situation where they were expected to 'look after' sisters in various ways. At one extreme were boys who agreed with the restrictions placed on their sisters and cousins and collaborated in the process by informing on them and advising parents to restrict them further. Others were more tacit in their approval of these restrictions. Some boys simply did not get involved. At the other end of the spectrum were boys who disagreed with the double-standard and supported their sisters and cousins in arguments with their parents. They enjoyed going out in groups, which included their sisters and cousins; although parents saw this as chaperoning, these boys did not.

During discussion on these issues, a pattern developed which suggested that the level of racism these boys encountered influenced their attitudes on these matters. For example, one boy who described how he had been bashed by members of his own football team in the changing rooms because he was the only Greek on the side, expressed extremely protective attitudes towards his sister. Many of these boys voiced a deep resentment of girls from their communities who went out with 'Aussie' boys. This stood in contrast to their own behaviour, as many stated that while they would not marry an 'Australian' girl they were happy to go out with these girls.

Ethnic majority girls felt that ethnic minority girls were over-protected and were glad that the same restrictions did not apply to them. They commented that ethnic minority girls did not like them and thought they were 'slack' (promiscuous). This was because they 'went out and had fun', were allowed to wear the clothes and jewellery they wanted to and dye their hair. According to these girls this created a jealousy and subsequent dislike of them by minority girls. They were resentful of the lack of trust in 'Aussies' that this over-protection implied. They also resented the standards of sexual decorum that were being set by these communities and against which they were judged unfavourably. They argued that if ethnic minority girls were not so cloistered, their own behaviour would not appear as extreme by comparison. They considered differences between what constituted acceptable female behaviour as a major obstacle in attaining intercultural harmony. This was as much a statement about the way they were viewed as it was about the way ethnic minority girls were treated. They made comments such as 'Girls are allowed out here' and 'Women have rights in Australia'.

The maintenance of reputation, in this sense, was clearly an issue unique to ethnic minority girls. Ethnic minority boys were unaffected except in relation to their role *vis-à-vis* their sisters. For ethnic majority girls, the issue of reputation also became relevant only in relation to the ethnic minority girls. It seemed to them that their behaviour was judged appropriate or otherwise against standards which were being set in relation to ethnic minority girls. They were being judged 'slack' because the ethnic minority girls were, in their words, 'over-protected' because their parents did not trust 'Aussies'. Ethnic majority girls confirmed this dichotomy by reserving their hostility for the ethnic minority girls and perpetuating their image of sexual purity, an image against which they were judged to be promiscuous. Thus, not only did the issue of reputation function to restrict ethnic minority girls' socializing outside school because of parental requirements, but also it created a division between ethnic majority and minority girls at school which further isolated the latter. Because of this, the ethnic minority girls were the most isolated within the pattern of school-yard interactions.

This same division between the ethnic majority and minority boys did not exist, despite the violence prompted by racism which both groups of boys discussed. On the whole this was due to the boys' mutual interest in sport. While both groups of boys stated that they did not socialize with each other out of school, they were happy to play sport together during school lunchtimes. In this way, while ethnic status and gender combined to isolate ethnic minority girls, it combined in the opposite direction for ethnic minority boys, who socialized with all groups of students. Figure 1 illustrates these students' descriptions of their school-based social interactions.

The interactions between these girls cast (in ethnic terms) the dilemma placed before adolescent girls in general. On the one hand, they were wishing to conform to the fashionable sexual image so much a part of popular youth culture and, on the other hand, they were needing to cope with the implicit social condemnation of this image. The ethnic boundaries, delineated by gender in this situation, were ones in which the ethnic minority girls were cast as 'good girls' and the ethnic majority girls were cast as 'bad girls'. Within these categories, however, the price for being 'bad' seemed higher for ethnic minority girls. Indeed, they also paid a price for being 'good'.

In the context of schools in working-class areas, where most students are

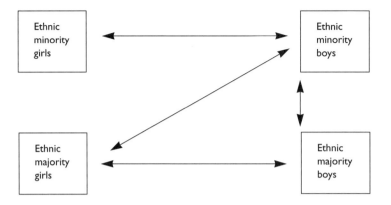

*Figure 1*   Social interaction in coeducational schools as described by students

from ethnic minorities, it is difficult to see any one group of students exercising control or benefiting from the complex articulations between gender and ethnicity. This is not to deny the unequal power relations that underpin these articulations. The interaction between gender subordination and racism illustrates that these factors are not cumulative or established in any deterministic relationship, but that each affects the nature of the other and both are responsive to context. It is clear, that the 'girl' in ethnic minority girls is different from the 'girl' in ethnic majority girls, similarly the 'ethnic minority' is different from that in ethnic minority boys. In relation to all of these students, ethnicity and gender combine to alter the nature of each element. My concern is not to reinscribe hierarchies of worth by inverting them. Nor is it to conclude in favour of the difficulties one group of students, experiences relative to other groups. My aim is to explore the role played by schooling in processes of identification, as these are both gendered and ethnicised. These processes are contingent and responsive to context as has been argued in Chapter 2. In the remainder of this chapter I wish to consider specific contexts as a means of detailing some aspects of this process.

## A girl's reputation

Specific social and geographic contexts are pivotal in determining a girl's ability to socialize in ways that both she and her parents find acceptable. I would like to illustrate this through a discussion of two groups of girls with whom I worked. One group attended a single-sex girls' school and was of Turkish extraction. The other was of Greek extraction and attended a nearby coeducational school. While both groups complained of being overly restricted, the extent of this restriction varied enormously between them.

The Turkish girls represented the most recently arrived group involved in this study. With the exception of two, these girls were born in Turkey and had arrived in Australia as young children under the age of 5. One girl had arrived in Australia aged 13 and another was born in Australia. Being a relatively newly arrived community, the individual families had financial preoccupations and were still in the process of acclimatizing themselves to life in Australia. In some instances the circumstances surrounding the family's migration were traumatic; for example, one girl stated that her father had signed papers which he thought committed him to becoming a guest-worker in Austria and instead found himself on a one-way trip to Australia. These girls commented that their families had not yet decided to become permanent residents of Australia and many were contemplating going back to Turkey to live. The majority said that their parents had regretted the move to Australia and that life here was not what they had anticipated. Significantly, none of these families had made a return-trip to Turkey since their arrival in Australia. For other communities, this had been the catalyst for their decision to settle permanently in Australia. The majority of these Turkish girls stated a clear preference for returning to live permanently in Turkey. A small number was unsure, and none stated a clear preference for remaining in Australia.

Within the school, these girls formed a distinct group based on their ethno-religious background. Turkish girls from various year levels socialized together and there existed a strong sense of solidarity, based on perceived difference from all other groups of girls. They attributed this difference to their religion and customs. Being Turkish and being Muslim were critical to their identification. Only one of these girls chose to wear a head-scarf and stated that her recent decision to do so was based on the desire to establish her rights as a Muslim. These girls argued that what separated them from other girls was the way they dressed, the way they behaved in public, the respect they showed for their elders and the way they socialized, particularly with members of the opposite sex. They illustrated these factors by contrasting themselves to their peers and pointed to the smoking, yelling, swearing, arguing with teachers and parents, the wearing of jeans, and the sexual overtones of the interaction they witnessed between girls and boys of their own ages, as the type of behaviour they found unacceptable. One girl characterized the situation as the existence of 'high mountains between us'. She wrote of her peers:

> At very young ages they go out with boyfriends, smoke, drink alcohol and do silly things such as kiss on streets, swear in public and hurt and abuse each other. If we as Turkish girls were to be seen doing such things, gossipers would say things that would make you kill yourself.

I worked at this particular school for over two years and in this time I witnessed these girls become increasingly Turkish-identified. Their interpretation of Turkish, however, was peculiarly inner city, adolescent female and almost 'punkish' in style. Many of them mixed elements of what would be seen as traditional Turkish clothing and jewellery, with the trousers, shoes and haircuts most often associated with inner-city, alternative youth culture. Although all of these girls had a good grasp of English, they chose to speak Turkish at every opportunity, including during class time. They cut out and pasted on their folders pictures of Turkish popular music idols instead of the British, American or Australian idols that other (ethnic majority and ethnic minority) girls displayed on their folders.

In an attempt to provide an affirming curriculum for these girls, the school applied for a special grant in order to employ an ethnic teacher's aide to promote Turkish language and cultural maintenance. The group developed a clear presence in the school, rebellious in its insistence on being Turkish and different. The involvement of the Turkish teacher aide with this group of girls created new opportunities for these issues to be expressed. One example of this was the screen-printing of windcheaters with the slogan 'I am a young Turk'. The double meaning implicit in this phrase captured the way these girls challenged the stereotype of the passive Turkish woman by insisting on their right and preference to maintain and reinterpret, rather than deny their culture.

As a group, these girls felt overly restricted and described how they were not allowed to go anywhere without a chaperone. This included going out during the day. The majority lived on a housing commission estate in close proximity to each other and other members of their community. According to these girls, the older women who lived on the estate were responsible for the restrictions, which they had to endure. These women took on the role of moral guardians for the community and watched the girls and gossiped about them and their families if they behaved in a manner which did not meet with their approval. Some of the girls stated that their mothers also found this situation stressful and for this reason their priority often became saving enough money to enable them to buy a house and move out of the estate.

These girls considered the restrictions placed on them as a product of life in Australia and this was the reason given by most of them for wanting to return to Turkey. Many were corresponding with girls their own age still in Turkey and argued that by comparison, their own lifestyles were more restrictive. Their socializing consisted of visiting members of their extended families and family events like weddings. This community was not well established and there was little evidence of support structures operating within it. Families who had been in Australia longer had already moved from the estate. This contributed to the lack of community-run facilities in the area, which could have offered support.

In contrast to this, the group of girls from Greek extraction were mostly born in Australia. All of them had been to Greece either for extended holidays or because their parents had decided to return permanently and had then resettled in Australia. They described themselves as Greek-Australian and discussed the way their trips to Greece had allowed them to recognize the Australian part of themselves and distinguish between themselves and their Greek-born counterparts. The majority of these girls expressed a preference for living in Australia even though they stated that while in Greece, they were allowed more freedom of action by their parents. Significantly, the one girl who felt most strongly about returning to live permanently in Greece was also the one who had most recently migrated to Australia and had not visited Greece since leaving.

Within the school these girls tended to socialize in small groups, mostly with each other but also with girls from other ethnic minority communities. As a community, the Greeks were well established and had been in the area for a very long time. There were churches and a large number of Greek community schools, restaurants and shops. Because of the number of Greeks in the area and because of the number of years they had been there, the community structures which had developed produced a more realistic reflection of variations among members of this community. Such differences reflected socio-economic factors, political and religious beliefs, regional differences and age groups.

Within this community most girls were grappling with the sexual double-standard related to male and female virginity at a philosophical level. While there still existed a need for these girls to protect their reputations, the sort of behaviour that would bring them into disrepute was quite extreme in comparison to the Turkish community discussed above. So while these girls, on the whole, were happy with the level of freedom they were able to negotiate with their parents, they were unhappy with what they considered to be blatant double-standards regarding codes of conduct for girls and boys. Generally, these girls participated in a range of social activities related to the school, the Greek community, their families and the wider community. A Greek-Australian youth culture had developed in this area and this was a significant factor in relation to the girls' ability to negotiate a social life that they and their parents considered appropriate. This centred around being allowed to go to discos on Friday and Saturday nights. What needed to be negotiated with parents was how often they could attend, with whom they went and what time they could come home. These discos were frequented mainly by Greek-Australian and Italo-Australian youth and although not organized by either of these communities directly, they were seen to be ethnic minority institutions. The Greek-Australian girls attended these discos in groups which included members of their extended families and friends. The fact that members of the family, particularly males, were with them, and the fact that these discos were attended more or less solely by ethnic minority youth, gave these girls and their parents a sense of confidence. The girls stated a preference for not socializing with ethnic majority youth, whom they described as violent, prone to drinking alcohol, swearing and taking no pride in their appearance. Although the boys in their families did not socialize in ways very different from the girls, the major difference related to the girls' perception, that for them, this level of socializing was a privilege, while for the boys, it was a right.

Although both the Turkish and Greek girls were dissatisfied with the level of restriction placed on their socializing, they associated this restriction with their minority status in Australia rather than their ethnicity *per se*. This is a subtle but important difference; that is, they suggested that life in their countries of origin would be less restrictive and their parents' current attitudes were a product of living in Australia where the general ethos was one they found threatening. These girls were proud of their ethnic backgrounds, and many described how the restrictions which they had to negotiate were evidence of their parents' caring attitude towards them. They thought that mainstream girls had total freedom and that this was indicative of their parents' neglect of them. They described, in overall terms, their enjoyment at being part of communities which were caring and offered them support structures and protective parameters within which to socialize.

## Aspirations

Some NESB parents don't want daughters to go to university in case they get 'Australianized'. There is a pressure on them to get married, often by proxy.

(Teacher)

Schools should get NESB parents to understand what kids are capable of. Daughters are seen as potential doctors by parents. They need to be told their kids aren't good enough without insulting them.

(Teacher)

University diploma opens every door in life – choices for freedom. Not like me who can't speak English and I'm given the worst jobs and conditions and treated badly.

(Mother)

Australian teachers say that migrant parents are too ambitious because Australians want to keep migrants as slaves – discourage them from going to university so they can get somewhere.

(Mother)

Captured in these comments are the contradictions evident in schools related to migration and the possibility of upward social mobility and the role of schooling within these. I am particularly interested in these contradictory discourses as they relate to gender. As evident in these comments, migrant aspirations are nuanced in particular ways when the students in question are girls. As has been stated previously, the aim within this project was to interpret this debate through the students. What were their aspirations? How did they understand their parents' aspirations for them? What was their conception of the role their schooling played with regard to their potential to achieve their aspirations?

During discussions related to migration, the ethnic minority girls stated that a major consideration in their parents' decision to emigrate was the study and work opportunities which they anticipated Australia would offer their children. While these girls linked study and work and saw it necessary to succeed academically in order to gain entry to prestigious vocations such as law, many of these girls also spoke of the value of an education quite apart from its vocational benefits. 'A good job' was a term used to encapsulate these beliefs. Such a job was one which had status because of the qualifications necessary or because it involved a worthy focus, such as helping people. Above all, such a job was clean and allowed people to maintain their dignity.

> My reason for migrating is that my parents had thought of my future in school, by the way my ambition is to be a computer technician. Although I wanted to be an archaeologist I have to pick computers because it's much more easier.
>
> (Dilek, Year 10)

> I believe being a lawyer/barrister is a job that is respected (perhaps) and something that is of high status.
>
> (Dorothy, Year 10)

Many of these girls discussed their parents' lives in Australia and the difficulties involved in the migration process.

> She [mother] has to work, leave her family behind, being separated from her daughter and grandchildren. Difficult for her to not understand English because at factory she cannot understand her friends.
>
> (Yucel, Year 10)

For many, their own aspirations were linked to the sacrifices their parents were making on their behalf. The difficulties of migration were recognized as worthwhile if they could achieve academically. Similarly, if they could achieve, their own lives would not be as difficult as those of their parents. In these ways there was a family investment in children's education. Most of these girls wanted to finish their schooling and a large percentage wished to continue on to some form of tertiary education, most commonly university. In fact ethnic minority girls, more than the other groups of students involved, aspired to university education.

In overall terms the ethnic minority girls nominated a disparate range of vocations which included both those which would be considered traditional and non-traditional for women. For example, the range included nursing, teaching, beauty and fashion-related work, as well as police work, horse training, politics and drumming in a band. Hairdressing, teaching and secretarial work were particularly popular with this group of girls. The range of vocations nominated by ethnic minority girls was the narrowest relative to the other groups of students.

The students were asked to list three vocations in order of preference and it is interesting to note the discrepancy between these individual choices. Rather than select three comparable vocations, for example, ones which all required a tertiary education, the ethnic minority girls would often nominate one vocation which required a university degree and couple this with hairdressing, for example. A pattern emerged whereby these girls would place the vocation requiring a university degree as their first or third preference; as their second preference, an adventurous choice requiring no formal qualifications, for example, one related to music, the fashion industry or politics; and one they considered attainable, often hairdressing or secretarial work, as their alternative first or third choice. During discussions, these girls explained that they were distinguishing between the vocation requiring a university degree, which was the one they preferred but felt they could not attain, and the vocation they felt they were able to attain.

This tendency to distinguish between preferred and attainable vocations was not apparent with the other groups of students. Generally, the other students showed a preference for vocations, which they considered attainable. This implies that ethnic minority girls could have been over-ambitious, lacking in self-confidence or ill-informed on matters related to careers, relative to their peers.

The girls discussed the aspirations that they thought their parents had for them. While many could not comment about the specific vocations that their parents, particularly fathers, wanted them to enter, they were aware of the type of work their parents considered desirable. Many summarized this work with the phrase 'a decent job'. Generally this meant a professional or white-collar vocation. The majority stated that there was no discrepancy between their parents' aspirations for them and those they had for themselves. In instances where such a discrepancy was seen to exist, the girls felt that their parents were overly ambitious for them, for example, one girl commented:

> My parents want me to be a doctor but they aren't forcing me to be that. They are the occupations which are needed more and easier to get a job if we go to Turkey. My parents' choice and mine is different because I think being a doctor is much harder and much more work.
> (Hafize, Year 10)

In many instances where this discrepancy existed, the girls commented that their mothers were particularly ambitious for them. These women were keen on their daughters having opportunities that they had been denied because of circumstances or because of their gender. According to these girls, their mothers also felt that the type of work they were doing in Australia, most often factory work, was particularly unsuitable for women and they did not want their daughters in the same situation.

Many of the girls thought that their parents wanted them to have a career rather than a job. Such a distinction was made on the basis of status, conditions and remuneration, as well as the notion that if someone had qualifications they could undertake work in another country or resume work after an absence with minimal career disruption. According to these girls, their parents were stressing the security they associated with qualifications. The girls commented that they saw no differences between the aspirations their parents had for them and those they had for their brothers. They felt that their parents were equally encouraging of both girls and boys finishing school and entering a high status career. Some girls did comment, however, that their parents would be more accepting of their sons than their daughters working in a vocation which was considered dirty, dangerous or involved outside work, for example, trades such as motor mechanics or carpentry. Moreover, this was an opinion most shared with their parents, for example, one girl commented:

> If I was a boy the jobs I picked probably would be different because I wouldn't want to sit in an office all day.
>
> (Hafize, Year 11)

With regard to career and educational aspirations, two characteristics were significant in distinguishing ethnic minority girls from other students. They were the only ones to distinguish between desirable and attainable career choices. Other students listed three careers choices, which were linked on the basis of similar status or direction.

The other important difference between the ethnic minority girls and other groups of students was their relative ignorance of prerequisites, rates of remuneration and duties involved in their career choices. Other students were able to discuss in detail the subjects necessary at secondary school, the range of post-school courses available and the number of years they would need to train or study. They could also discuss in relative detail the type of work that their career choices involved. Many had stated that they had discussed their career choices with a wide range of people, including family members other than their parents, teachers and friends. This was not the case with the ethnic minority girls who, on the whole, said that they had discussed these issues only with their mothers.

Ethnic minority boys were similar to the girls discussed above, in that the majority wanted to finish school and go on to tertiary education, with university education a common aspiration. Many nominated professions such as law, engineering and medicine. Many of these boys included trades in their career preferences. The most common were hairdressing and motor mechanics. As a group, these boys included a wider range of career choices in their preferences than did the ethnic minority girls and more of them aspired to becoming self-employed in a business of their own. Like the ethnic minority girls, these boys were aware of their parents' aspirations for them. This was exemplified in one boy's comment that, 'My parents want me to have a job where I don't have to slave like they have.' Most felt that if a coincidence did not exist between their own aspirations and those of their parents for them, this was because their parents were being overly ambitious.

Mostly, ethnic majority girls had lower aspirations than both ethnic minority girls and boys. A smaller number of them aspired to finish school and go on to tertiary education and a smaller number still included a university education in their aspirations. On the whole these girls chose careers that they thought required in-service training or pre-service training for which it was not necessary to complete school. Child-care work, nursing, secretarial work and veterinary nursing were popular choices in this category. Fewer aspired to trades given that, unlike the ethnic minority girls, hairdressing was not a popular inclusion. Relative to the ethnic minority girls, these girls seemed better informed about the prerequisites, duties and remuneration rates associated with their choices. Unlike the ethnic minority girls, there did not exist a discrepancy between their preferred aspirations and those they felt were attainable. Thus, the minority who aspired to a university education and a professional career, as well as those who wanted to do secretarial work or nursing, all felt that they would be successful.

In the main, the ethnic majority boys were the group of students who included trades in their career choices. Unlike the ethnic minority boys and girls they did not include hairdressing in their selection but concentrated on trades like plumbing, carpentry and electrical work. They thought that these careers were not suitable for women and as a result they were the only group of students who aspired to work they considered unsuitable for both women and men. These students seemed well informed about the prerequisites, duties and remuneration rates associated with their aspirations and many stated that they had already spoken to people involved in this type of work. As a group, the ethnic majority girls and boys differed from the ethnic minority girls and boys in that most of them stated that they were either unaware of their parents' aspirations for them, or that their parents did not care what they did.

## Aspirations, migration and class

As has been argued, one of the aims of the committee which established this project was to respond to the themes that arose out of *Girls, School and Society* with regard to minority girls. I have accordingly presented material from the study around themes related to educational and vocational aspirations and gender relations. As has been stated, this study was established to consider these issues in the broader context of these girls' life experiences, particularly those related to migration and class and to do so through centring the girls' perspectives.

The schools selected for the study were considered by the Victorian Ministry of Education at the time as disadvantaged. This status was determined on the basis of a range of indices including parental income and occupation and percentage of non-English background enrolments. Such schools were eligible for extra funding to support additional programmes, which would benefit these groups of students specifically. Between the schools involved, these additional programmes included school camps and a pet programme. These were developed to provide the students, many of whom lived in high density, high rise, government subsidized housing, with outdoor recreational activities and an opportunity to care for animals. Schools also subsidized excursions and one ran a breakfast programme. Students came from low income families and many had parents who worked long hours or shift work. Some of this additional funding was also earmarked by the national government for the employment of ethnic teachers' aides. This was an acknowledgement that parents with limited English language skills needed support to enter the life of the school and ethno-specific aides were employed to assist with such community liaison.

Migrancy does not have a straightforward relationship with class and traditionally, children of migrants who settle in working-class suburbs enter university in higher numbers than their mainstream peers. This has often been attributed to the aspirations implicit in migration. However, this relationship also is not straightforward. These issues will be explored further in Chapter 5. The intention here is to provide some detail for the argument made in Chapter 3, that the conception of ethnic minority girls which dominates educational discourses is one which fails to take account of their class location and the impact of the migration process. Are girls kept home to look after siblings because their families and cultures are particularly patriarchal or do families with few economic resources and many needs because of migration, including adults with few English language skills, rely on children more so than most? On the issue of domestic work, much like on the issue of going out, all students regardless of ethnicity and gender recognized the double jeopardy involved in being a girl. Within all families there were expectations that girls do more than boys. It is likely that in situations where there is more work to do, girls will have to do more.

Ethnic minority girls reviewed much of the dissatisfaction with their lives in the context of life in Australia. For most of them this included a range of hardships and hostilities which were a product of the migration experience and their minority status.

Both parents had to work. I had to look after two brothers four and five years younger than I when I was 10 years old and I hardly saw my parents. Lack of community involvement. Generally entirely different environment/lifestyle.

(Michelle, Year 7)

I began interpreting for my mother at an early age. At 7, my knowledge of Italian was poor, especially when I had to interpret in front of doctors and teachers. When doctors began to use their jargon I wondered to myself what they were talking about. Also the only Italian I knew was the Calabrese dialect.

(Connie, Year 12)

These girls outlined the loss of family networks, the cultural alienation and dislocation, the shifts in their relationship with their parents and their added responsibilities brought about by migration.

These ethnic minority girls were concerned with the racism that they and their families experienced within Australian society. They discussed this in relation to their parents' employment, their own schooling and the social interaction between members of their communities and the ethnic majority. There was an underlying assumption in many of their comments that they and their communities received unfair or unequal treatment because of their ethnic status. Sample comments include:

I know they call me a 'wog' – but it doesn't worry me, I'm proud to be a 'wog'.

You want to know everything about them and you want to be like them so that you won't be called a 'wog'.

Working at an old age in a hard labour. Working in a country where he [father] cannot communicate because he can't speak English.

They [parents] often say that they wish that they were educated so they wouldn't be treated like 'dirt' by the boss.

The students' comments illustrated that the migration experience and its consequences altered in response to gender. Comments made by all groups of students indicated that a larger share of domestic responsibilities fell to girls, regardless of ethnic background, and similarly, that relative to boys, all girls had more restrictions placed on them in relation to going out. However, both these issues were also affected by migration, drawing clear distinctions between the ethnic minority and majority girls. For example, ethnic minority girls commented about translating and interpreting for parents, paying bills, looking after younger siblings and doing housework because their parents could not speak English, because they had to work overtime, lacked other support structures or were unfamiliar with alternative options. While boys undertaking the same type of duties may have been reluctant to talk about this, it is generally acknowledged that girls, regardless of ethnic background, are expected to do more home duties and that migration exacerbates this because children have added responsibilities (Schools Commission 1975a).

## Sameness, difference and racism

Despite the fact that within these schools, ethnic minority students constituted close to or over 50 per cent of the overall student population, many ethnic minority students complained of racism and accused staff as well as other students of this. While the categories, non-English-speaking background and English-speaking background, have grave limitations both in terms of reconstituting binaries between real and non-real Australians and submerging differences within each category, such categories, none the less, had a real presence in the minds of the students who participated in this study. The labels commonly used by these students to constitute these categories were 'wog' and 'skip'. 'Wog' is traditionally a pejorative term used in reference to members of southern European minorities in Australia. More recently it has been recast, particularly through so-called 'ethnic humour', as a term of affirmation. Students used it in this latter sense in reference to themselves and in opposition to the 'skips', a term derived from *Skippy the Bush Kangaroo*, a somewhat dated Australian television serial featuring a young boy and his pet kangaroo named Skippy. While these students did not recognize ethnic differences within the 'skip' category, they used the term 'wog' to refer to a range of ethnicities. These included Greek, Italian, Serbian, Croatian, Lebanese, Turkish and Maltese.

Ethnic majority students also lived this divide. These students were vocal about their preference to be at a school where all students were like them. They could see no advantages in having students from diverse cultural backgrounds at their schools and when asked to comment on this issue in the wider context of Australian society, were limited in their response. The following comments are illustrative:

> They are nicking all the Aussies' jobs.
>
> (Laurelle, Year 10)

> They take over everything we have got, they run all the jobs. And they seem to get a lot more money than we do.
>
> (Michelle, Year 10)

> They get money once they hit the tarmac and get a nice car.
>
> (Jason, Year 10)

Jobs straight away, free money as a gift as well as the home-buyer's grant.

(David, Year 10)

Aussies learn different cultures and foods while wogs get a job, a car, a house and another Aussie is out on the street. Some people who were once on the poverty line now live under it because of wogs, slopes and chings.

(Anonymous)

They make our cars, they grow our plants so I guess they are doing us a good favour.

(Lorraine, Year 10)

The strength of this divide was most evident when students discussed potential marriage partners. Minority girls voiced the preference for marrying within the 'wog' category; within this, only religious differences between Muslims and Christians were nominated as significant. Minority boys were most concerned to marry within their particular ethnic group and gave as the reason for this the wish that their children be brought up within a family that maintained their mother tongue and culture, a responsibility they identified with the mother. Minority girls also saw this as an aim but felt that this was possible for them within marriages where the father was of a different ethnicity, as long as he shared with them a 'wog' background. With few exceptions, majority boys and girls also expressed a desire to marry within their 'Aussie' group.

Particularly during adolescence, schooling represents the congruence of a range of issues fundamental to processes of identification. Emerging sexualities, manifestations of femininity and masculinity as these are interpreted through youth cultures and dominant images, relationships with parents and families, responsibilities related to academic and vocational futures are all crucial for these young people. For most of these ethnic minority students, their parents' decision to emigrate was based on the desire to provide their children with more life opportunities. Education was understood as a major means of facilitating this. However, this decision brought with it a range of hardships including the type of employment undertaken, the breakdown of support systems and extended family networks, the experience of racism and loss of status, communication difficulties and participation in a social milieu that many found threatening to their value systems. The assumption that they were second-class citizens extended to their participation in the education system.

Added to this, many of these girls were attempting to fulfil high aspirations, which (to some extent) migration had created through the promise that their attainment was possible. Yet the experience of schooling, for most, offered evidence of their low status within the Australian community. Most understood their schooling to be sub-standard and believed this to be so because they were in 'migrant areas'. They also described systemic sexism, expressed at school through sexual harassment, restricted use of facilities and limited subject choice. The following comments are illustrative of these issues:

> I want the teachers to teach us more.
>
> (Anonymous)

> The majority of students don't want to cooperate. The Education Department refuses to give more money.
>
> (Tina, Year 10)

> I have to struggle against teachers and pupils to gain a serious working environment. I think there is too much mucking around. That means I can't get my work done at school.
>
> (Dorothy, Year 12)

> Sometimes I like school because it's nice and some people are kind but sometimes I don't like it because it is boring. Some boys smack us and when we go to the toilet there is smoke and some people in our class are naughty so we can't play. I don't like the uniform and I like radios to bring some music. I hate maths and history and English. Some girls think they are top dogs but they are not. I want the principal to tell the boys to stop spitting and I want the canteen to be a bit big and I want decoration with flowers.
>
> (Rosanna, Year 7)

> I hate some guys because they always talk about the woman's body.
>
> (Olivia, Year 8)

> I don't care if I had a male teacher but some look at girls' bodies.
>
> (Anna-Maria, Year 7)

In overall terms, the experience of schooling was not positive for these girls. It was important to them and they wanted to be successful; however, they remained pessimistic about the potential of their schooling to help them attain their aspirations. Under these circumstances it is likely that such girls require additional resilience to maintain an interest in and have success with their education. Over and above all the other issues in their lives this may be a tall order indeed.

The discussion here is based on the experiences of girls from countries which could broadly be described as southern European. They are also the stories of girls who were born overseas or whose parents were born overseas from the country where they now live. These girls were also those living in areas associated with lower socio-economic status. The relationship between migrancy and ethnic status is a complex one, particularly with regard to academic achievement and upward social mobility. In Chapter 5, these issues will be explored through a shift in emphasis. The next study that will be discussed began in 1994 and included some of the same ethnic groups. This study also included Chinese, South African and Russian groups. These groups represent more cultural and socio-economic diversity as well as more variation with regard to length of residency.

# 5 'Good' students and 'good' schooling

In this chapter, I discuss a study funded by the Bureau of Immigration, Multicultural and Population Research begun in 1994. The Bureau, a Commonwealth-funded body, provided commissioned and other research on issues implied by its name. The intention with this project was to explore patterns in educational achievement in relation to what the Bureau described as immigrant background groups. A range of issues including fields of study, course type, place of birth, ethnic background and gender were explored. The study had both quantitative and qualitative components. The quantitative element used statistical data to provide a national mapping of tertiary, mainly university education. On the basis of this mapping, key groups of students were isolated for the qualitative phase of the study. Students from these groups were interviewed in ethno-specific, single-sex groups in a variety of schools in Melbourne and Brisbane. This was done in an attempt to understand factors that contributed to their success or otherwise in accessing and participating in university education. In this way, it was intended that both the presences and the absences would be read and a picture formed as to what school-based factors help or hinder educational attainment of this kind. (More details related to this study are provided in Appendix 2.)

Similar to the study discussed in Chapter 4, this study was established by a government committee concerned broadly with multiculturalism. Again it was a somewhat defensive response to a particular policy debate. Traditionally, affirmative action strategies within the tertiary sector have acknowledged both gender and ethnic minority status as worthy of attention (DEET/NBEET 1990). More recently, however, there has emerged an argument about the declining necessity for such strategies for both these categories of students. This has been argued on the basis of enrolment figures, which have been interpreted to indicate an equal, if not higher level of attainment for these groups (Birrell and Khoo 1995; Birrell et al. 1995; Dobson 1996).

## Immigration and education

The role of immigration and its concomitant aspirations and the impact of these on academic achievement have been long acknowledged and debated (Taft 1975; Marjoribanks 1978, 1980). In the 1970s the view that children of immigrants would not be disadvantaged educationally, which had hitherto dominated, had been challenged (Martin 1983). The experiences of teachers and their advocacy on behalf of minority students as well as demands made by minority communities eventually led to the establishment of the Child Migrant Education Programme in 1971. This programme initially emphasized the acquisition of English but increasingly responded to pressures that this be integral to a range of issues including mother-tongue maintenance, bilingualism and multiculturalism.

Educational opportunities have been linked to upward social mobility. Coming to Australia for a better life has meant not only the material rewards for work – the house in the suburbs, the car, the furnishings and white goods – but also the chance for children to become educated and enter professions where status would accompany economic security achieved through less arduous means. As early as 1978, the Galbally Report identified that some groups were less likely to make a successful transition from school to work (Committee of Review of Post Arrival Programs and Services to Migrants 1978). This concern has been exacerbated by the restructuring of the Australian labour market in the 1980s. Numerous studies indicate that in relation to unemployment, overseas-born young people who stay at school are more likely to be unemployed than their peers who leave school early (Miller 1984; Sheldrake 1985; Cahill and Ewen 1987; Miller and Volker 1987).

This link between education and the aspirations of migration has been debated with particular strength as it relates to the children of immigrants. In the early to mid-1980s the debate focused on notions of disadvantage relative to discrimination. Commentators such as Birrell and Seitz (1986) argued that immigrant communities were well if not overly represented in tertiary education. Because of this it was inappropriate to refer to them as disadvantaged. On the contrary their achievements needed to be highlighted. Theirs was an experience that could be linked to alternative work ethics and an exemplar of how barriers related to cultural capital could be overcome. On the other side of this debate, commentators such as Jakubowicz and Castles (1986) and Kalantzis and Cope (1987) argued that rather than define immigrant communities in relation to disadvantage, there needed to be an understanding of discrimination as a means of analysing educational attainments.

In relation to this debate, several communities receive specific attention. The Turkish, Arabic, Maltese and South American communities are most often associated with a lack of educational success regardless of length of residency (Cauchi 1987; Inglis *et al.* 1992; Inglis 1993). The debate has considered causes, such as discrimination, or in some cases, the assumption that there is limited success itself has been challenged. With reference to the Arabic community specifically, for example, Kisrwani (1989) argued that within NSW there was a disproportionate number of Arabic youth leaving school early and without formal qualifications. This has been attributed to these students being stereotyped by Australian teachers (Al Anwar 1989).

These debates are about categories and how they are constituted as much as they are about numbers. We have to understand not only that terms such as educational success are slippery but also the limitations of categories such as 'Arabic'. Abu Dunhou and Teese (1992) pointed out with reference to this community, the shortcomings of capturing significant diversity in one such term. Within 'Arabic' are constituted Egyptian, Lebanese, Palestinian and Syrian backgrounds. Within these there is religious difference, different migration experience and experience as it is gendered. These authors found that Australian-Egyptians, for example, had greater participation rates in higher education than Australian-Lebanese. They also noted that female educational participation was relatively low within both communities.

## Categories and common sense

More recently, these debates have been revitalized in relation to policy concerned with equal opportunity and affirmative action, particularly within higher education. Reflecting shifts in immigration patterns, these debates have focused on recent minorities, particularly those constituted as 'Asian'. Given this, these debates are also intermeshed with the historical racialization of ethnic minorities such as Chinese people. The traditional construction of such groups as 'unassimilable' and a potential threat to the Australian way of life stands in contradistinction to the shifts in public discourses about the need for Australia to engage more creatively with its Asia-Pacific neighbours as discussed in Chapter 2. More so, since education, particularly higher education, is increasingly seen as a key Australian export in this region. These complex and contradictory discourses are being played out in Australian classrooms and have consequences within higher education.

The commonsense view of the Asian student stands at the opposite end of the spectrum to that commonly understood in relation to Arabic students. In a similar vein 'Asian' is used to conglomerate a vast difference based on migration experience, ethnicity and socio-economic status. None the less, the image is one of studious and successful students who devote themselves to study and have a strong association with maths and sciences. There have been indications that within this group many do experience academic success, such as Chinese background students (Bullivant 1988). However, as with 'Arabic', 'Asian' has to be nuanced to account for diversity. For example, in a study conducted by Teese *et al.* (1993) there were indications that in the working-class, western suburbs of Melbourne, Chinese and Vietnamese students were experiencing little academic success.

In overall terms, the debate about education, aspirations, migration and ethnicity is labyrinthine. It meanders variously through generalities and specificities. In some cases contextualizing factors such as class are taken into account, in other cases there is a simple conflation of migration with ethnicity. Most glaringly, within this debate, diversity within generic categories based on factors such as gender, ethnicity and religion are accounted for inconsistently. In such a context, there is little possibility of making comparative judgements within or between the categories. In fact, the categories themselves become increasingly suspect. For me, this debate provides a framework within which questions are produced rather than answered. Mostly, this is because of the constant reinscription of these categories in so much of the policy and research literature. In this regard, the Bureau Study was no exception.

In the lexicon of the funding body, the research was to examine 'immigrant background youth'. This was an attempt to account for students born overseas in English-speaking and non-English-speaking countries and those born in Australia often referred to as 'second generation'. The databases used for the quantitative component of the study relied on government collected statistics. These categories sometimes contradicted themselves, for example, the placing of Turkey in both Asian and European categories. More fundamentally, however, the figures compiled for university participation relied on Australian students nominating a language spoken at home to determine ethnicity. Such processes are fraught with difficulties. Birthplace is not the same as ethnicity, nor does language always coincide with ethnicity. Additionally there is great variation in the rates of mother-tongue maintenance. Importantly also are the vexed politics of ethnic labelling, through self-attribution, through communities and through institutional discourses. The debates surrounding these issues as they relate to processes of identification will be explored further in Chapter 6.

A critical aim within the Bureau Study was to explore school-based factors which may help to explain the patterning of higher education enrolments in relation to place of birth, language spoken and gender. Additionally, the intention was to provide alternative stories by looking behind the often quoted figures for tertiary entry. This has particular salience with regard to debates about gender. In Australia, as elsewhere, attention has been paid to the rising number of girls who complete secondary schooling and enter university. Such figures are used to indicate the diminishing need for specific programmes for girls and in some cases, to argue discrimination against boys. Because of the 'what about the boys?' debate, as it has become known, there is increasing interest in tertiary entrance figures and how these are played out with regard to course type and field of study and in relation to post-study options (Yates and Leder 1996; Kenway *et al.* 1997; Arnot *et al.* 1998; Lingard and Douglas 1999).

The Bureau Study was an attempt to engage with the debate about ethnicity and that related to gender. It was also premised on the understanding that neither of these issues could stand alone and on the contrary were intermeshed in ways that affected both debates. One of the intentions in this study, particularly through the qualitative work, was to explore, not whether girls were doing better than boys, nor whether ethnic minority students were doing better than their peers were. Instead, it was to explore which girls and which boys were doing well and which minorities were doing well. What were the meanings attributed to 'well' and what were the schooling experiences of those students who did and did not do well?

Ten groups were identified for the study and the choice reflected much of the preceding debate related to commonsense understandings of which groups achieve and do not achieve. On the basis of statistical data, a range of groups considered well and poorly represented at the tertiary level were determined. Selection from within this range of groups was made on the basis of a range of factors. These included the level of establishment within the Australian community of particular ethnic groups. Perceived ethnoculturally specific attitudes to educational attainment were considered. Recency of arrival and educational experience prior to migration were taken into account. Additional demographic features including representation within the population generally and specifically within universities were also considered. Attention was also paid to whether or not particular communities had been previously researched. The groups selected were Italian, Greek, Turkish, El Salvadorean, Polish, Russian, South African, British, Chinese and Vietnamese. In this chapter I discuss some of the implications of this study on the basis of the qualitative work undertaken in schools. It is important to note that while the categories of students were determined in the way described above, the allocation of students to these categories within schools was based on their own self-attributions.

## 'Good' students

As mentioned, the Bureau Study took place at a time when academic success in relation to categories of so-called disadvantage was coming into question, particularly in relation to gender and ethnicity. With regard to ethnicity specifically, this was linked with the so-called Asianization of Australian universities. In the logic of those who found increasing participation of students identified as Asian a problem, it was explained variously in relation to the internationalization of Australian education and a particular work ethic with which Australians could not compete. The relationship between academic aspirations, expectations and experiences of schooling and racism was considered specifically in the study. In particular, the image of the 'Asian' student as conservative, diligent and high achieving was explored. In the context of debates and stories within the media of high-achieving Asian students, students within the schools were asked to identify the category of students which did well and some of the reasons for this. Every attempt was made to couch this question in terms that did not immediately imply ethnicity. Very few students, however, discussed this issue in relation to other factors. Those who did made reference to gender or class. Every attempt was made to keep these discussions as open as possible and students were asked to define 'good' in their own terms. Invariably, a good student was associated with the capacity to pass exams and receive high marks, which would facilitate entry into higher education, particularly university. When it came to identifying which students were good in these terms, in general, the responses took one of two forms. Students either identified particular groups of students and then described their academic characteristics, or identified academic characteristics which they associated with academic success and then linked these to particular groups of students.

The following comments provide some insights into students' responses when asked to identify the type of student who did well at school.

Those who are nerds – people who spend all night working.

Students who are more about their work than their social life.

Students who believe that an academic life is better than a social life – nerds, dags and geeks.

> (Group of South African girls from a private Jewish school)

There are some Australian kids who do very well.

There are no nations who only do well or badly.

Australian parents don't care what their children do.

They must be the best parents. Really cool.

European parents care. It comes down to the attitudes of the parents. Our parents will support us.

> (A group of Polish boys from a state school)

The Chinese have a high work ethic and stricter parents.

It depends on which group you associate with – there are groups who are doing better or not. Students from Eastern countries have parents who are very strict. The harder you work the more money you will get. The Asian parents say if you are working hard you are getting something done.

In a couple of generations it will be there. We will have the same expectations for our children. It is a matter of what kind of people you are.

> (A group of Chinese boys at a state school)

Students from Taiwan, Hong Kong and China may do better because they have a good moral training.

> (A Chinese boy at a language centre)

Students whose parents push them, who don't have many friends and who don't have many distractions.

They don't talk – are not popular.

They are boring with no sense of humour.

Anyone who is daggy.

> (A group of Greek boys at a state school)

More boys do well than girls. Parents are scared for girls. They don't want them to get boyfriends. If a girl gets a boyfriend then they get boy mad at school and they don't concentrate as well.

> (A Greek boy at a state school)

Many of the Asian kids do very well, not all of them however. They put more effort into their studies. They don't socialize. They are committed to their studies in their country. Their learning system is very hard. Also, many of them are very poor and they want to do better.

> (A Polish boy at a state school)

Taiwanese students because:
>   They are ambitious.
>   They work quickly.
>   They had good maths education.
>   In Taiwan used to a lot of homework and exams.
>   I want to do my best as do my friends.

Australians:
>   Some well educated ones.
>   They have excellent English.
>   They organize their English work.
>   They are enthusiastic.
>   They feel the pressure from us and don't want to be left behind.

> (Group of Taiwanese girls at a state high school)

Students who have parents who care for them very much.

Asian because:
>   They are favoured by elderly people.
>   They are made to study day and night.
>   They are grateful for a good education.

> (Group of British girls at a state high school)

The link between migrancy, aspirations and an alternative work ethic is clear in these comments. So too is the association of these factors with 'Asianness'.

This understanding was common to the various groups of students involved in the study, including those within the Chinese and Vietnamese groups. Similar attributes were associated with relatively recently arrived Polish and Russian students. However, not all recently arrived students were associated with these attributes.

The South African students made comments about 'migrant' students doing well but tended to associate this term with Russian and Asian students. While these students were themselves born overseas they did not refer to themselves as migrants. This seemed typical of the understandings attributed to terms such as 'migrant' (discussed in Chapter 2) related to being 'foreign'. The South African students involved in this study were English-speaking on arrival, and most lived in relatively affluent suburbs and attended a private Jewish school. Many of the Russian students interviewed also attended this same school. However, their circumstances were very distinct. The relationship between the Russian and South African students will be discussed in more detail in subsequent sections of this chapter.

El Salvadorean students were also one of the most recently arrived groups included in the study. In most cases these students were born overseas. However, while these students associated academic striving with migrancy, they too linked this to Chinese and Vietnamese students and not to themselves.

Gender was mentioned within rather than across categories of students; for example, some Russian girls felt that girls did better than boys because they worked harder. In the context of exploring 'good' students, gender was rarely mentioned. Similarly, class was rarely mentioned. When it was mentioned it was not associated with specific groups of students on the basis of ethnicity. Comments were broad, linking 'good' students with their parents' capacity to employ tutors for them or purchase computers. One El Salvadorean boy commented:

> The ones who don't have economic problems do best. Their parents give them economic support. Too many students have had to drop out to help their parents because they are having economic problems.

## 'Good' but not 'cool'

There were a number of issues, which became intertwined in the comments of these students. Definitions of migrancy and academic success seemed to be related but not in straightforward ways. Similarly, academic success and being 'daggy' or 'nerdy' were ethnicized but again not in straightforward ways. These issues related to class and gender but in ways that did not readily form patterns. In summary, the following themes developed from the interviews. 'Migrants' were students who did not speak English or who were deemed 'Asian'. Chinese students, for example, regardless of birthplace and the capacity to speak English on arrival, were deemed 'migrant'. In this way, the characterization of 'migrant' coincided with 'foreign' variously ascribed through lack of English language skills or 'Asianness'. Some 'migrant' groups were associated with academic success but not all. Such academic success was attributed to a particular work and study ethic, which in turn was associated with a hunger for upward social mobility. This hunger was understood in relation to a previous lacking of some sort. 'Asian' and Russian students, in particular, were seen as fleeing poverty and oppression. These same groups were also associated with education systems that were highly structured and competitive in their countries of origin. Similarly they were associated with parents who were austere and demanding. These factors combined most commonly with reference to 'Asianness' to produce 'daggy' or 'nerdy' students.

It was in the context of describing 'good' students that many created a binary between academic competence and being fashionable or 'cool', that is, successfully interpreting popular youth culture. Of most interest here is the fact that students, across all the schools involved, associated particular ethnic groups with academic success. This is significant because through it, not only was academic achievement ethnicized, but also, by implication, so was being 'daggy'. Comments made by students from a range of ethnic groups indicated that a strong dichotomy between the academic and the fashionable existed within the cultures of their schools. The Chinese and Vietnamese students, for example, situated themselves and were situated by others on the 'daggy' and academic side of this divide. What the Chinese and Vietnamese students saw as the need to work in order to achieve and the support of their families for this endeavour, other students characterized as either the product of their repressive family situations or their inability to socialize and have fun in ways understandable within school-based renditions of mainstream popular culture. Another illustration of this same dichotomy was furnished by one group of El Salvadorean students who situated themselves on the social and fashionable side of the divide. These students described themselves as underachieving academically because they preferred to go out, have fun and be fashionable. As one girl put it:

Spanish students do badly. They are slack and want to have fun.

## On being 'Asian'

One of the aims within the Bureau Study was to engage with the debate, current at the time, related to the so-called Asianization of Australian universities. In this context, Chinese and Vietnamese students were considered a priority for a range of reasons. At one level these students were understood as academically diligent and successful in accessing university education.

This perception was verified during the study. Other students often referred to 'Asians' when exemplifying the model student, regardless of their recency of arrival.

Within the Bureau Study the Chinese and Vietnamese students were considered a priority because they remain the groups commonly racialized in Australia (as discussed in Chapter 2). There was an interest to consider their schooling experiences in relation to the possible impact of this racialization. What is the possible relationship between racialization, the construction of 'Asianness' and how 'good' students are understood? The vehicle for exploring this issue will be these students' understanding of what constitutes a good education. By asking the students to explore this, the aim was to consider their estimation of Australian schooling as well as their attitude to schooling more generally.

Within Brisbane, forty students (twenty-two female) who identified as Chinese were interviewed. These students were born in Hong Kong, Taiwan and the People's Republic of China. The majority stated that they spoke Mandarin at home. All were born overseas and had lived in Australia between one and nine years, with most having lived in Australia between five and six years.

Within Melbourne nine students (eight female) who identified as Chinese were interviewed. Seven of the Chinese students were born in either Malaysia or the People's Republic of China and had lived in Australia between one and fourteen years, the majority over ten years. One was born in Australia. With the exception of this student, who stated that English was the language spoken at home, the majority of the remainder identified the home language as either Mandarin or Chinese.

Within Brisbane twenty-five students (thirteen female) who identified as Vietnamese were interviewed. These students were all born overseas, spoke Vietnamese at home and had lived in Australia between one and fifteen years, with the majority having lived in Australia between two and three years.

Within Melbourne schools, fifty-one students (thirty-eight female) who identified as Vietnamese were interviewed. One of these students was born in Australia; the rest were born overseas and had spent between one and ten years in Australia. Of these, the majority had lived in Australia over five years. One student identified Laotian as the language spoken at home, while the rest spoke Vietnamese at home.

## Good schooling

### Vietnamese girls

Vietnamese girls felt that a 'good' education should provide, as two students stated, 'achievement of good knowledge' and 'up-to-date knowledge'.

English and Vietnamese language skills were clear priorities. In many instances, these students refered to social communication skills. There was a preference for a broad rather than specialist curriculum. Most also referred to the need for schooling to provide a range of life skills, including independence skills, social competence, better career education, driving lessons, experience about society, self-confidence and friendship. One girl summarized this range of issues as 'preparation for life and work in Australia, becoming a good citizen, being able to distinguish between right and wrong'.

Many girls focused on the need for teacher professionalism with some coupling this with the comment that teachers also needed to be friendly and caring.

Resources and facilities were a focus for discussion for many. Comments centred on the need for good equipment, especially computers, better equipped libraries and more quiet study areas. Some girls also mentioned better canteens with healthier foods.

In some contexts, these girls commented on the need for a friendly environment in which they did not experience racism. For many of these students, this was associated with the need for stricter rules enforced more diligently by staff.

*Vietnamese boys*

These boys stated a preference for a wider range of subject choices. They stressed the need for knowledge towards a degree or certificate and as one boy put it, 'more serious subjects for students'. Subjects mentioned specifically by this group of students were English and mathematics. These students were concerned with education as preparation for a good job with a good earning capacity. None the less, they were interested in an education which provided knowledge related to 'respect for society' and 'morals'. Preparation for good citizenship and future life in Australia were mentioned by many.

In general, these boys advocated what they saw as a better approach to education where some students' bad behaviour did not affect the learning of others. In this context, one boy suggested the need for good teachers and good students who would improve the academic climate of the school. In this context, some students commented on the need for more discipline, advocating suspension and detention for misbehaviour. In one context, some boys referred to the need for better teachers, and a school environment which was 'peaceful and clean' with no alcohol or drugs. Many of these boys argued the need for better buildings, facilities and equipment, particularly in science rooms.

*Chinese girls*

These girls stressed the need for a disciplined learning environment and student motivation. Many comments elaborated these desires in terms of the need for 'sufficient work', 'fairness and strictness'. Most of these students focused on the role of the teacher in the provision of a 'good' education. Some commented on the need for teachers who were more dedicated and in this context the comment was made that there should be 'no teacher who has favourites'. One group of girls suggested the need for 'Asian teachers to help Asian students'. Their education results were seen clearly as a product of how the teacher behaved *vis-à-vis* support, provision of work, providing students with motivation and discipline. In some contexts, these students stressed English language skills above all else. Few mentioned social skills or friendship in this context. However, some did stress the need for moral education.

English language skills were mentioned by many, particularly those at the language centres. Other specific subject skills referred to included computer education and some girls mentioned study skills.

Many of these girls expressed a desire for better facilities. Most often mentioned in this context were library facilities and the need for more books and quiet study areas. Some girls wanted freer access to the school building during non-class times.

These girls also articulated a preference for a more disciplined environment where students took more responsibility for school facilities. Comparing Australian schools to those in Taiwan, one group of students mentioned the need for students to clean the school themselves, thus saving expenditure on cleaners and contributing to a better school environment.

*Chinese boys*

Many of these boys felt strongly that a 'good' education was one that provided a clear link with work through mechanisms such as 'practical work experience with big companies'. Many also stressed the need for students to develop a range of personal skills such as goal setting and the capacity to be 'a good person' through what many referred to as 'moral education'. Some boys stated that the role of schooling was to 'provide wealth by moving students out of poverty'.

In one context, these boys were disgruntled because the school had recently 'crossed out' Chinese language from the curriculum and felt that this was due to the fact that Australian students did not want to compete with Chinese students in this subject.

Some of these boys argued the need for better-qualified staff and smaller class sizes. In several contexts, students argued that 'some teachers are racist'. Some also mentioned the need for better facilities and equipment and a 'good study environment'. For many of these boys, such an environment was linked to students who were disruptive and teachers' capacity to contain such students.

In response to other questions, it became evident that these students found the academic aspects of previous schooling experiences more rigorous. Many stated that their study of maths overseas meant that they were able to excel in related subjects in Australia. Most also contrasted their attitudes to academic work to those of other students. They felt that their attitude was more serious and family supported this. Many of these students identified this attitude to work in general, and school work in particular, as part of being 'Asian'. Some suggested that it was common to other 'migrants'. In general terms, this distinction depended much on the school these students attended and the other students with whom they had contact. For example, in one context, the students identified Asian and Russian students as having the same ambitions and attitudes.

In terms of gender differences, these seemed fairly muted among the Vietnamese and Chinese students. Two differences that emerged related to a stronger focus from the boys on the nexus between schooling and work; comments from the girls that they perceived boys from their communities more susceptible to distractions at school and in some contexts Vietnamese girls commented on boys joining gangs. Yet despite such minimal differences between these girls and boys, on the basis of 1993 national figures, the Vietnamese community had the lowest participation rate for females in the tertiary sector of the ten groups studied, that is, 43 per cent of Vietnamese students at university were female. This contrasted to 50 per cent for the Chinese group.

### Racism

The issue of racism is clearly relevant to the way ethnic minority students experience schooling. The Chinese and Vietnamese students who participated in the Bureau Study made reference to racism in various ways. Many commented on the need for more discipline at their school as a means of containing racism. Additionally, some commented that their teachers were racist. Perceptions of racism and how it is constituted remain complex. Through schooling racism is depicted through subtle and obvious ways. It relates to what is taught and how it is taught and assessed. Racism is enacted through teacher–student relationships as well as relationships between students, and teachers and parents. Students understood the importance of parents to the schooling process and the link between their parents and their schools. One El Salvadorean student, for example, commented that there should be 'more assemblies for parents' in her argument that schools should construct this link actively. Drawing on material from the Bureau Study I shall describe some of the complexities related to racism as these were described by four groups of students. Various schools are involved and the groups of students represent different experiences.

### Chinese and Vietnamese students

As discussed in Chapter 2, non-indigenous minorities deemed to be 'Asian' are most vulnerable to racialization. Comments made by Chinese and Vietnamese students confirmed this vulnerability. Within these groups, students commented on the racism they experienced, to the point where some boys referred to physical violence against them. At one school, a single-sex girls' school, Vietnamese girls interviewed were particularly vocal about the issue. Some of their comments included:

> My parents don't really know about the school. They have approached the school and the staff have been very impolite. There have not been enough letters. The teachers are racist.

> A good school should not be racist. The parents ring the school and the school is very rude. It is important that the school is polite.

> How we get on with the students depends on us. Some students are racist. It depends on how we take action. If they are racist and we ignore it and don't do anything it is our fault.

> Some of the teachers are not friendly to everyone, some teachers treat Australians better. Some teachers have problems at home and let them out on us. The teachers should be more understanding. Teachers don't always help us when we have problems. Some of them are racist.

These comments indicate a range of issues including school–parent liaison and how this is understood by students, student–staff interactions and interactions among students.

Newly arrived students who attended intensive language centres also commented on racism. The following comments were provided with the assistance of an interpreter working with Chinese-speaking girls at a language centre. Considering what made a school good, these girls commented that there should be no racial discrimination. They wanted an atmosphere where all students could communicate happily. One student recounted what had happened to her aunt in a school where her things had been stolen, she had been spat on and sworn at and even had things thrown at her. They expected racial discrimination when they left the language centre. They thought that some people might not express it but that they had it inside them.

One group of Taiwanese boys at a secondary college projected this sense of vulnerability into the future. In this context, the comment was made that there would be no work available for Chinese in Australia because it was a racist country and that because of this, some of these boys anticipated returning to Taiwan after completing their studies.

### Russian and South African Jewish students

A group of Russian Jewish boys with whom I worked at a coeducational Jewish college provided an example of a different form of racism. This school had recent enrolments of Russians and South Africans. These Russian boys described the racism they encountered on a daily basis at the school. Having fled an anti-Semitic environment, they and their parents chose to integrate themselves into the Jewish community, yet within the school, it was their Russianness that had become the focus for attention. The ways in which these boys described their daily experiences of name-calling, isolation, victimization from staff and (I would argue) response to this through creating a unified group, were reminiscent of the experiences of the Turkish girls at the single-sex school described in the 1984 study. It was particularly noteworthy that some of these boys spoke with great passion about the way the 'Australian' girls, in particular, treated them. I was left with the strong impression that although the treatment meted out by these girls was not worse than that of their male peers, the Russian boys found it most humiliating and that part of this related to the sexual dynamics involved. Only one boy was explicit about this and commented that these girls would never go out with him because he was Russian and they thought they were better than him.

In the context of this Jewish school one of the markers of these students' experiences related to definitions of Jewishness. Some boys found the environment overly stifling. They gave examples of this, including the requirement that no meat could be brought to school as a way of ensuring the implementation of Kosher eating codes. Another boy commented that the school should offer Russian language, not just Hebrew, which was compulsory. During this discussion an interesting division became evident among these boys. Some boys argued that they had a more liberal interpretation of Jewishness by preference. This involved less ritual, few restrictions regarding food and less emphasis on Hebrew. In this context, one boy stated that he was not circumcised and did not understand this to be an issue. On the other hand, some understood this liberal interpretation of Jewishness not as choice, but as a product of the anti-Semitic Russian environment within which they had lived prior to migration. For this group, it was an exemplar of their oppression.

As mentioned, this school had enrolled numbers of South African students. During discussions with one group of South African girls, their comments about the Russian students were particularly pertinent. In their minds the Russians were a clearly defined subgroup within the school. This was attributed to a range of factors including their relative recency of arrival and their limited English language skills. While these South African girls were also immigrants, they arrived speaking English. There also existed a resentment on the part of some of these girls because they understood that the school, through their own fees, was subsidizing the fees of the Russian students. These girls also described the Russians as 'thinking of themselves as different', 'isolating themselves', 'sticking to themselves' and 'making themselves victims'. This was the most liberal end of the spectrum of descriptions used for the Russian students, the other end of the spectrum included comments such as 'smelly Ruskis'.

In the context of this school, the Russian students were described in terms associated with 'Asian' students. These students were 'migrant' and had the associated work and study ethic. During discussions this group of boys commented that 'immigrants do best at school especially Asian and Russian migrants' and 'immigrants are used to working hard in their old countries and come over here and do the same'. 'Russian students do best at school because they work the hardest.'

*Turkish girls*

The third group of students I wish to discuss specifically were Turkish girls at a coeducational state school, which enrolled a large number of Turkish students. Special provision had been made so that the uniform would comply with Islamic dress codes. Girls could choose to wear their school skirt at a particular length and a specifically designed head-scarf was also available. While not all the Turkish girls chose to wear this version of the uniform, many did. Nearby to this school was the mosque which the community attended and allied to this, an Islamic independent school. There existed divisions among the Turkish community at this state school, related to levels of Islamic orthodoxy. At the time of the study, the Turkish community liaison officer employed by the school was organizing meetings with Turkish parents in an attempt to resolve the school-based manifestations of these differences.

Turkish girls from this school who were interviewed for the study complained about racism and victimization and named staff as well as students as perpetrators. These girls commented that girls who wore the long skirt and head-scarf were particularly vulnerable. Within the school, they were referred to as 'nappy heads'. With particular reference to staff, these girls argued that they received less attention, were given lower marks and fewer chances if they failed to meet requirements, such as getting homework in on time. The girls illustrated their argument by describing comments made to them by staff which included 'You're dumb – you won't get anywhere anyway' and a particularly poignant comment, 'Go home and do some washing'. During this discussion I asked these girls whether they had made their parents aware of this situation. Most responded that they had not discussed this matter with their parents because of their reluctance to cause trouble. Those who had stated that their parents had advised them to avoid trouble and one way of doing this was not to speak Turkish or talk about Turkey at school.

*Greek students*

The fourth group of students were Greek girls and boys attending a coeducational state school. These students argued that they experienced racism and in their comments were understandings of racism, similar to those of the Turkish girls described above. They too argued that teachers victimized them by not giving them as much help and being less flexible when it came to requirements. At this school, some of these students were concerned about what they understood as their teachers stereotyping students and making assumptions about them on this basis. Comments were made about inadequate support from teachers. One girl reiterated her teacher's statement when she asked for assistance as 'Not you again'. A boy at the same school stated: 'I feel like a marked man . . . when they [teachers] see the name, they will only give an average mark.' Students were asked to comment on what changes to the school they thought their teachers would advocate and in response to this question the following comments were made: 'Get rid of Greek students', 'think that Greek students are a pest'. These students felt that they were not receiving adequate support for their studies and were aware that their parents could not provide the support that could assist them. One boy commented:

> [It's] difficult to take responsibility for correcting own grammar mistakes – very difficult to speak Greek at home and not at school. Parents cannot help at home, more often teachers push us away and only brothers and sisters can help.

Again the school's capacity to communicate with minority families was perceived as important by these students. One girl commented that the school no longer sent newsletters home in Greek and other home languages. School reports went home only in English. These students argued that as a result, their parents had very little contact with the school. Other girls in this group argued that this minimal contact was the fault of the students because they did not tell their parents about the school. As a result their parents did not find out what was going on.

The manifestation of racism within schools may not conform to commonsense expectations. The examples discussed here have been selected to illustrate how readily made assumptions about racism may not coincide with its lived reality. While school demography is a significant issue, it is not always the case that large numbers of students from the same community attending the same school will reduce the likelihood of racism, as in the case of the Turkish girls. Nor can it be assumed that students who share some similarities are not divided by intra-group differences. Even in situations where a shared identification in response to particular forms of subordination, as with the Jewish students, differences within this category can have dire consequences. At another level, we cannot assume that groups commonly racialized will automatically experience school-based racism. The Chinese and Vietnamese students who attended intensive English language centres, for example, found the environment comfortable and the staff extremely helpful, and it seems that their interactions with other newly arrived students caused them few difficulties in this environment. Yet these students anticipated that this would not be the case when they left the language centre and the comments from students with similar backgrounds at schools seemed to confirm their projections. Additionally, it cannot be assumed that well-established communities, such as the Greeks, are not also vulnerable. There exists a common understanding that groups such as those from southern Europe face less racism. Often this is attributed to the fact they are no longer considered newly arrived immigrants and that factors such as familiarity, assimilation and intermarriage have played an important role in the diminution of racism. This assumption warrants further examination.

In this context, it is also worth considering that racism may not always take an overtly negative form. Discussing racism directed towards 'Asians' in Australia, Hage (1998) describes the attitude as a 'neurotic imaginary' which relies variously on negative features and ones which are excessively positive. The latter he argues 'also works to dehumanise the "Asians" and make them appear as if they are superhuman' (Hage 1998: 221). I would conclude that the characterization of 'Asian' students within schools as the epitome of the 'good' student, in the terms discussed above, is a further example of this.

## Educating for the 'new times'

Because of its core and compulsory nature, schooling represents a form of institutional practice and a range of discourses which converge with processes whereby students form cultural understandings of who they are and their place in society. This relationship can be particularly significant during adolescence. How individuals see themselves relates to how they are seen by others. This is a dynamic and complex process, more so in an ethnically diverse country like Australia.

Students' schooling experiences form a bridge between mainstream society and the culture of their family, between the public and the private spheres of their lives. Through it, students learn where they fit in, how aspects of their home cultures are represented within and evaluated by the Australian education system and by implication, the wider society. The curriculum, both formal and informal, becomes a statement about how students are perceived, how their aspirations are understood and what assumptions are made about their identifications.

For both girls and boys from ethnic minority backgrounds, there has been exploration of processes of identification as these relate to educational access, experience and attainment (Tsolidis 1986). Indications are that for minority students, there can exist a significant lack of congruence between what is assumed by schooling as valuable knowledge and what it is they bring with them to the classroom. The school yard provides lived experience of cultures of worth. In the classroom, the language, the ways of teaching and learning, and importantly, methods of assessment, provide mechanisms for reward which are critical to future opportunities and ways of seeing oneself. Schooling, as it mediates the private and the public, provides students with a significant context for negotiating their subjectivities.

How we understand education and its role in processes of identification is increasingly shaped by globalization. Understandings of ethnicity, definitions of 'Australian', who accesses education and to what ends, are all issues which must be examined as they emerge out of a global market, culture and communication system. In this context, notions such as ethnicity become increasingly problematic. What is the basis on which we judge ethnicity and what is its relevance in relation to national boundaries and understandings of citizenship? These issues are particularly pronounced in a country like Australia where a history of migration has made terms such as 'Australian' contentious in themselves. More so than ever before, the possibility of a crisply delineated Australian category is under scrutiny. This situation is exacerbated with time. There are the children and grandchildren of immigrants, the children of mixed marriages, there are multiple migrations, remigration and the conscious decision made by many to live between two countries. National boundaries and the ethnic groupings which exist within these are constantly reinterpreted, not only by migration, but also related to this, global economic structures and communications and a global popular culture.

In this context why attempt a study circumscribed by what some would argue are outdated understandings related to ethnic identifications? In part this is because while the context may be changing, the response to it can be a further consolidation of narrow, hegemonic understandings of ethnic and national identifications. In Australia there exist strong commonsense understandings of who is Australian. Globalization has instilled in some a desire to reinscribe these understandings. In this context, education plays a critical role, not only as a vehicle for definitions of Australianness but also in relation to who can and should successfully access the opportunities education can make available. One response to this situation is to deny the categories, another is to recognize them, despite their many shortcomings, as part of a strategic politics of identification (Spivak 1993); a politics which seeks to maintain a broad and dynamic definition of Australian and underpin it with an adherence to principles related to equity.

### Educating the 'new ethnicities'

Ethnicity has been traditionally conceived of as linked to inclusion and exclusion within collectivities established through a common feature associated with birthright. Increasingly, such seemingly straightforward definitions have been problematized. How do we judge the ethnicity of someone who was born in Australia to parents who were born in Italy? How do we judge the ethnicity of someone who was born in Australia to parents who migrated respectively from two different countries? How do we judge the ethnicity of someone who was born in Russia to Jewish parents from the Ukraine who now lives in Australia? Or how do we judge the ethnicity of someone whose family actively chooses to live between Australia and Hong Kong? While globalization, with its increasingly fluid national and cultural boundaries, at one level homogenizes, at another level it makes differences more familiar. 'Australian' no longer exists as a category associated with a British heritage, interrupted by the familiar post-war immigrant groups. Instead Australia, along with many nations, faces the challenge of interpreting citizenship through the cultural fluidity which is the result of globalization.

The familiarity of difference brings into sharper focus many of the issues surrounding notions of citizenship and nationhood (Castles 1997). In this context, ethnicity can be linked only to a form of identification which is voluntary and shifting. It is insufficient, either because of a willingness to include or the aim to exclude, to link ethnicity to nation. For an Australian raised within a Greek cultural framework, being labelled Australian can be as oppressive as being labelled Greek. The context for such labelling is of paramount significance and determines the power relations which underpin the exercise and the ease with which an individual can accept, reject or reinterpret the labels.

Within the study discussed here, the notion of ethnicity was explored in a framework which conceptualizes it, along with factors such as gender, as part of a process of identification which is shifting in response to context (de Lauretis 1990). A major intention was to understand the processes that students used to determine for themselves (and others) ethnic and gender identifications and how these processes interrelated with each other and the institutional practices and discourses of schooling. A significant component within this framework was the interpretation of students' aspirations and experiences in the context of the levels of attainment for the groups from which they came. Levels of attainment were established using data premised on the mechanisms used by government bodies to determine ethnicity; most commonly birthplace and language/s spoken. This was clearly problematic with regard to minority students who were born in Australia. For this group of students, data related to language/s spoken at home can become an indication of various rates of mother-tongue maintenance among ethnic groups, rather than ethnic background. Alternatively, for groups such as Spanish speakers, it is difficult to ascertain from such data whether their ethnic identification relates to Spain or a range of Latin American countries, for example. The qualitative component of the study, however, was premised on the ethnic self-attributions of the students involved. Most significance is attached here to this material as it is linked to the understandings of identification explored above.

Within schools, there were no misgivings about understanding students as Turkish, Greek, Chinese or Polish. The task of this identification was left to each school community and mediated by the relevant teachers. Researchers asked teachers to invite students, regardless of place of birth, to self-select as from particular ethnic groups. Most awkwardness surrounded the formation of the UK groupings. With the exception of those who were born overseas, the link between 'Britishness' and 'Australianness' was evident in the fluidity of identification between these groups. In itself this process has provided an exemplar of the continuing importance of processes of ethnic identification as these operate within Australian society. The challenge is to reflect on these in the context of changing understandings of Australianness and shifting theoretical interpretations related to these.

Processes of identification are interpreted and reinterpreted through institutional practices and discourses associated with schooling. How students see themselves is as much a reaction to their cultural backgrounds, their families, the processes of migration, as it is to the ways in which they are seen by friends and teachers. Schools represent a powerful interpretation of 'Australian' through the formal and informal relationships they mediate between people and their cultures as these are represented through discourses related to ways of understanding and ways of doing. In the context of schools students learn what it is to be Australian, who it is who is allowed to claim this label and whether or not they wish to challenge or accept mainstream understandings of these issues.

In similar ways, the institutional practices and discourses of schooling frame understandings of femininity and masculinity. These mediate the ways in which students confirm, deny or reinterpret gender representations through formal and informal curriculum, peer cultures and mainstream cultures. Students' capacity to create gender identifications respond to the power underpinnings of the many social interactions they experience. Critical among these, in Australia, are those concerned with ethnicity. For boys and girls from all ethnic backgrounds, self-identification processes reflect the articulation of their gender and ethnicity as these are expressed through the power relations mediated by schooling. In this study, significance is given to educational aspirations, experiences and attainments (as already discussed). It is not unusual for teachers and students to understand these aspirations, in particular, in ways which are both gendered and cultured. There exist strong commonsense understandings of the aspirations that Chinese boys, for example, bring with them to school and the reasons for these. These are understandings which exist as a reading of what it means to be a male within Chinese culture as this is interpreted within mainstream Australian culture.

## Combining the fashionable and the academic

In similar ways, school cultures interpret and define notions such as edu-
cational success and the possibilities for this. At an anecdotal level there is ample understanding of the distinctions that students can make between the fashionable and the academic. These understandings are gendered and cultured; for example, the positioning of academic success and sexual desir-
ability as opposites, particularly for girls, or the understanding that 'Asian' equals academic achievement and this does not coincide with being fashionable or having a good time.

Almost at a gut level, strong understandings exist of who does well at school, who enters universities and what types of courses various groups prefer. It is common, at an anecdotal level, to hear teachers and tertiary educators make statements exposing beliefs about ethnic groups, their prefer-
ences, their aspirations and their achievements. 'Asian' students prefer business courses. Turkish girls are not interested in (or not allowed to contemplate) tertiary education. Jewish, Greek or Chinese students are over-
represented in universities, particularly within law and medical faculties. Maltese and Lebanese students have low academic aspirations and relate more readily to the world of small business. These are familiar, if not empiri-
cally based, understandings of what goes on within ethnic minority com-
munities, and it must be considered that such judgements inform a range of practices, particularly within schools, which could determine the range of options such students can avail themselves of in the future.

While it is important to consider particular ethnic groups and their characteristics in relation to educational participation, it is also important to consider how these groups experience education. The ways in which groups of students understand their schooling can also provide insights into their attainments. Without this reciprocity we may be creating a situation where there is inadequate reflexivity with regard to the appropriateness of the existing educational provision, instead, focusing solely on the capacities of particular groups to adapt to or cope with schooling as it currently exists.

It is primarily for this reason, that the examination of the relationship between schools and the tertiary sector in this study was school centred. A major consideration has been to explore school-based practices as a means of understanding these data. What happens in schools which can help to explain the university figures? Furthermore, the school-based material has been centred on the experiences and aspirations of the students as these are interpreted by them. Once students enter or do not enter universities their academic fates are, to a great extent, sealed. It is what happens to them at school and the basis for this which has much more determining power. In schools, their academic experience is shaped by factors much less in their control and much more responsive to preconceptions of them which may exist. How do we understand the students we teach when we are faced by a group of students who are labelled Russian Jewish boys, or newly arrived Poles, or Turkish girls? Within this equation what is the relationship between their aspirations, expectations of schooling and ours as these are reflected back to us through our commonsense understandings of who the students are and what they and their parents want from life in Australia?

In relation to ethnic minority students and educational attainment, aspirations and experience, the challenge is twofold: first, to recognize intergenerational mobility as it relates to particular ethnic groupings as these become less obvious due to factors such as intermarriage and less distinct linguistic and ethno-cultural characterizations; and second, to consider the migration experience as a phenomenon with consequences for all immigrants and particular consequences for those with relatively distinct ethno-cultural profiles.

Can it be argued that for some groups, being newly arrived is good for educational attainment? What is the relationship between assimilation and educational aspirations? What is the relationship between reasons for migration and educational attainment? Are there factors, such as a presumed work ethic or an estimation of the worth of education, tied to particular cultural understandings, which in turn influence educational participation? How are attitudes to education shaped and in turn respond to students' capacity to deal with racism?

The role of popular culture in the context of schooling has a relationship with racism. One of the markers of racism is the silence within popular youth culture of those groups perceived of as culturally distinct. While this may disadvantage these students in relation to their school peers, is it an advantage in relation to their academic profiles? This dichotomy between academic and popular culture, as it was expressed by these students, is worthy of exploration in relation to culture and racism more generally.

Stuart Hall reminds us that there can no longer exist an innocent view of the 'popular' in popular culture. Instead, he describes the continued dialectic between the affirming notions implicit in 'popular' and the tendency for these to be coopted and subordinated by existing power relations. He argues that by its very nature, popular culture is a contested and contradictory space: 'There are always positions to be won in popular culture, but no struggle can capture popular culture itself for our side or theirs' (Hall 1996a: 470). Instead, he suggests, we evaluate popular culture in relation to the moment at hand. He elaborates this with regard to the black implicit in black popular culture and argues that it has become overdetermined.

We need to consider these arguments in relation to ethnic minorities within popular culture as it is expressed in the Australian context. It would be difficult to recognize the ethnic minority in this popular culture. As has been discussed, in the Australian context, cultural difference is minimally represented. It seems that at this particular moment, inklings of cultural difference which could be accused of overdetermination are few and far between.

The groups interviewed through the Bureau Study were diverse and (as has already been outlined) represented groups with various lengths of residency in Australia. Similarly, their academic achievement was varied. What is more, no direct link could be argued between this length of residency and academic achievement. Instead, however, a link could be tentatively argued, between groups with high academic achievement and an historic diasporic experience, such as exists with the Greek, Chinese and Jewish communities.

It was striking through the interviews, how students from these communities had a clear sense of who they were and the relationship between this and their academic aspirations. To various extents, what was particularly noteworthy in this context was these students' descriptions of alternative forms of youth culture which were embedded within their minority cultures. This was particularly so with the Greek and Jewish students. It is worth considering this historic diasporic experience as a means of challenging the dichotomy between academic and peer-based social success. Perhaps it is the existence of diasporic youth culture which allows such students to create a third space (Bhaba 1983) between academic and popular cultures, particularly at a moment when the popular is defined so narrowly. It is in this context that we need to return to the articulations between gender and ethnic identifications. These interconnections are as important to processes of subordination as they are to the creation of alternative representations which challenge their hegemony. The repertoire of racism and gender and class subordination fuel and are fuelled by commonsense understandings of ethnic minority women and their communities. However, there is a need not only to challenge those representations that subordinate, but also to consider gendered power relations within the third space. As educators, we have to consider the role that schooling plays and can play in providing all students with opportunities to reflect upon, reinterpret and create cultural understandings which enable them to juxtapose the academic and the social aspects of their lives. This will be discussed in more detail in Chapter 6.

# 6   A feminist praxis of difference

The two studies I discussed in Chapters 4 and 5 were framed by my engagement, at the time, with various debates within feminist theory. In this chapter I wish to consider these debates, their relationship to each other and to the overall aim of the book. This is to explore as transformative schooling that creates a dialectical relationship between equity and difference.

The Educating Voula study was framed by the feminist theoretical debates of the 1980s. These provided great comfort for those in the margins in the process of constituting themselves as subjects, demanding to be heard and making public their opposition to the deficit-based, hegemonic images of them being constructed by others. This study was established by a committee with the responsibility of providing the Minister for Education with advice on multicultural education. It was part of an era that many thought could constitute a policy-led educational revolution. An element of this revolution was a system of committees which were said to be representative. It was through these committees that many parents, unionists, women and members of ethnic minorities entered decision-making processes. In this spirit, the sponsoring committee for this study included members of ethnic communities who were formally constituted as representatives of these communities. This was a great shift in emphasis for prior to this, such committees had few members of ethnic minority communities and framed their concerns in relation to 'migrant' education which was understood, primarily, as English language tuition. After many years of being commented upon by others, within frameworks which understood ethnic minority status in deficit terms, the sponsoring committee developed this study in ways which sought to privilege the standpoint of ethnic minority girls. In this context, it was important that I, as researcher, was also from an ethnic minority community.

During this study, I conducted classes in several schools over a two-year period. The classes were made up of ethnic minority girls and through these, the issues which developed as important for these students were then presented to groups of boys from similar backgrounds and girls and boys from the mainstream. It was a methodology which was unapologetic about centring these girls on the basis of their traditional marginalization in both the educational discourses concerned with gender equity and those concerned with multiculturalism.

In this framework, being positioned as a feminist researcher working within schools on the educational experiences of minority girls was, theoretically, relatively unproblematic. I was working to voice the hitherto silenced. My research was school based, enacted through teaching, and was guaranteed a policy outcome by virtue of its sponsorship by a government body. Here then was an exemplar of feminist praxis, of knowledge contributing to a practice of change and vice versa.

In 1994 I began the Bureau Study, again funded by a government body concerned traditionally with migration and, more recently, with multiculturalism. The Bureau had a reputation for privileging quantitative research related to demography. Not surprisingly, the study was established to include a quantitative component analysing government databases. Unlike the Educating Voula study, it had not been framed in ways that privileged minority standpoints nor overtly emancipatory outcomes. This study was described as an investigation into the attainments of 'migrant background' students.

The Bureau Study was framed in the context of a very different theoretical climate. Gone was the comfort of speaking for and from the margins. Instead the scepticism surrounding the constitution of such locations and the privilege implicit in the inversion of hierarchies of worth – that is, the epistemic privilege of being relatively more oppressed – had consolidated itself. In my opinion, this was coupled with an impending inertia with regard to the types of research I valued and still value. While the shift away from the theoretical understandings which had been the basis of the 1984 study were ones I found convincing, I none the less felt lost with regard to the type of research these shifts could instigate. For colleagues in other faculties, particularly those associated with literary studies, I detected an uncomplicated synergy between full-blown post-structuralism and the research with which they were engaged. At the time, women's studies conferences that I attended seemed (to me) like an endless series of deconstruction; the more obscure the text, and the more obscure the tropes, the better it seemed (Tsolidis 1996b). How was I to frame a project, funded by a government body that insisted on a quantitative component to the study, around categories that were determined by the language of the bureaucracy, and maintain some semblance of theoretical dignity?

At one level, my desire to enter into this project was prompted by all the less than noble imperatives that are increasingly pressing in on academic work (research money, research quantum and the profile of the faculty and the university). At another level, I was genuinely interested in pursuing some of the issues that had surfaced through the Educating Voula study. I was still basically interested in working in schools, with students, in ways that I felt had the potential to engage with real-life debates about equity and education.

As a result of my understanding of these theoretical shifts and my inability to reconcile them through the practice of research, I argued for the utility of strategic feminist research. Such research could engage with the policy debates of the time, regardless of whether this meant it would be framed by the understandings implicit in these, including those about how knowledge is produced (Tsolidis 1995b).

How can I draw on this impasse as a means of reflecting on feminist knowledge production and furthermore use it in ways that may shed light on how we understand the schooling experiences of minority girls? In my mind, the link here relates to the politics of knowledge production. In academic research, in school classrooms, as elsewhere, what is considered worth knowing and the best ways of representing this, is attached to political processes determined by uneven power relations. Attempts to disrupt existing systems of authority risk reinscribing them or replacing them with new ones, which may not be more worthwhile.

Traditionally, feminist researchers established their authority to speak on the basis of the epistemological relevance of experience – the notion that the personal is political and also a foundation for theorization. In my case, working as an ethnic minority woman to speak the language of silenced minority girls seemed straightforward enough, in fact, had this not been the premise of so much feminist research to date? Yet there was an in-built contradiction in attempting to speak for a range of minorities constituted within the category 'ethnic minority' in order to destabilize the uniformity implicit in the category 'girls'. Was this a repetition of the same issue but at another level? To add to this dilemma, when I turned to the work of minority feminists to clarify this contradiction, it was they who sought to challenge the essentialism implicit in labels such as 'woman' which had formed the foundation of mainstream feminism, and yet it was they who also stood in strongest opposition to the dismantling of subject locations advocated by poststructuralism.

## Dismantling the different in the name of post-structuralism

It is this dilemma that I wish to explore here because (for me) it is this dilemma that speaks to how we work with both equity and difference. What we teach and how we teach it is fundamentally about politics – what knowledges and methods of constructing these have dominance. How then do we provide students, alienated from mainstream constructions of such knowledges, with affirmation for their existing knowledges? How do we do this without establishing a toothless pluralism or a form of equity which creates a strait-jacket in order to discipline difference?

The issues raised here are ones that contemporary social theory takes as a central problematic. They capture concern centred on the status of the subject and the concept of identity. In broad terms, the myriad voices that have been heard from the margins decrying the assumption of a unitary subject within structuralist discourses as a form of imperialism, have created an intellectual climate in which any subject location is considered sceptically. Although many of these marginal voices are themselves reluctant to relinquish the status of the subject, a momentum towards this relinquishment has developed which, to some extent, they have none the less precipitated. There are two levels of the same debate which will be explored in this context. One relates to the marginal voices which have brought the issue of difference to the mainstream arena and the other relates to this mainstream arena, within which the marginal are often still silenced, even though the debates are about difference.

Not surprisingly, I am drawn to the work of feminists who have a similar reticence to relinquish the notion of a political project because it is by definition framed by potential, if not actual, essentialist understandings of identity. Instead, they search for ways of reconciling the utility of identity and its increasingly untenable foothold in our ways of understanding.

In her discussion of postmodern epistemological politics, Yeatman (1991) argues that there exist two views of postmodernism, the view of the master subject and that of the Other; the women, natives and colonials who have precipitated the present crisis in western social science through their persistent challenge to its epistemology. Of particular interest to Yeatman are the feminists concerned with the politics of difference. Rather than being outside postmodernism, she situates writers like Anzaldua (1987), who are deeply concerned with issues of identity, within postmodernism. Yeatman (1991) does not link the politics of difference with the cultural relativism embedded in pluralism or liberal politics. Instead, she argues that feminists, concerned with difference, pursue identity politics within frameworks which understand power and the nature of domination. In this way she links them to a postfoundationalist epistemology, which in order to contest colonized subjectivities 'can proceed only by contesting the subject/object relationship which is inscribed within the discursive order of foundationalist science' (Yeatman 1991: 10).

It is on this basis that Yeatman develops her notion of postmodern critical theorizing. In this, she argues that modernism and postmodernism, rather than being oppositional, form a dialogical relationship with each other, as do colonialism and postcolonialism; that is, each is developed in and through the other. She contrasts positivist and critical interpretations of postmodernism to argue that the latter is different from a 'nihilistic relativism and anomie' (Yeatman 1994: 10). Instead she points to its potential to open up 'a democratic politics of voice and representation, where the ideal state is not the overcoming of domination once and for all but ongoing imaginative and creative forms of positive resistance to various types of domination' (Yeatman 1994: 9).

Spivak (1993) approaches the same considerations through the concept of a strategic politics of identification. She does not attempt to construct the possibility of an unessentialized identity. Instead, she argues that there is always an essentialism implicit in identifications, even those of a strategic nature. Her aim, however, is to examine the risks involved in the use of such esstentialisms. The major risk that she identifies is that of strategic essentialisms becoming lasting ones. She argues that rather than consider the strategic nature of such essentialisms and the risks involved during the euphoria of victory, these considerations need to be the preliminary basis of political action. She advocates a self-conscious use of masterwords like Woman, Worker or the name of a nation, by all those mobilized under such banners. One of her key points is that the tools of deconstruction must be applied to political masterwords before, during and after the mobilization that occurs around them. For deconstruction to be useful, she argues, it needs to be applied, not only to those things we oppose, but more importantly to those things we hold dear.

Most commonly, it is left to minority feminists to reflect on the short-comings of considering their own (in)visibility. In many ways, this constitutes part of the double burden of racism; that is, the question of (in)visibility itself and the question of what is to be done with this question. While there is a need to be self-conscious about the framework, the need, the cause and the outcome of engaging with this question, one has to be careful not to enter a state of political paralysis brought about by a disjuncture between the issues as these are lived and their theorizations. As Brah (1996) states, there is a need

> to think through the opacity of experience; to understand the relationship between subjectivity and 'collective experience' . . . experience does not reflect a pre-given 'reality' but is the discursive effect of processes that construct what we call reality. But then, how do we think about the materiality of that which we call real?
>
> (Brah 1996: 11)

## Collective experience

These questions recur at two fundamental levels. As a feminist researcher I am interested in understanding processes of change. I am also interested in collective experience as part of this change process. Being from an ethnic minority, one of my concerns is with the collective experience of racism.

Spivak's (1993) notion of strategic identifications is useful in this context. She places an onus on us to deconstruct the labels we hold dear as well as those we oppose – hence my attempts to review 'feminism' as it is understood in educational discourses through the collective experience of ethnic minority women and girls in Australian schools.

Many antiracist feminists have shown a reluctance to relinquish the notion of identity, and instead have sought to establish identity in ways which do not presume essentialized qualities. They have given identity a political interpretation, which to a great extent, is an expression of their adherence to the concept of praxis; that is, the belief in theory functioning to both reflect and express the concerns of oppressed communities, as well as function as a basis for their liberation struggles, a key element of which is antiracism (hooks 1981, 1984, 1989, 1990; Collins 1990; Huggins 1991; Huggins and Saunders 1993; Brah 1996).

These issues resurface time and again and as such must be reckoned with. Notions of visibility, the ability of the subaltern to speak, the epistemological relevance of experience, political identity, the contradictions between representations and the lived experience of racism, are all issues with which antiracist feminists engage, albeit in critical and self-reflexive ways, in the context of post-structuralist theorizations of subjectivity (Spivak 1990; Young 1990; Mohanty 1991; Bannerji 1993; Chow 1993; Spivak 1993).

While many feminists are critical of epistemological frameworks which valorize experience and are underpinned by notions of moral outrage, in the light of minority feminists' experience of oppression and their reluctance to forgo such frameworks, the question must be put: is the questioning of such frameworks a luxury which minority feminists cannot afford? The multiple and interrelated oppressions experienced by the communities which such writers theorize, their strong identification with these communities and their own experiences of these oppressions, create an imperative for political struggle which seems to characterize their work. This differentiation, in itself, constitutes an argument against the ability to dispense with experience and moral outrage in epistemological terms. This imperative for political struggle, framed as it is in relation to some form of subjectivity, leads such antiracist feminists either to maintain a commitment to a form of humanism despite the significant challenge that post-structuralism represents to this (Collins 1990), to seek non-essentialized notions of black identity (hooks 1990) or to consider the strategic imperatives of essentialism (Spivak 1993). This reluctance to sever the link between identity and political movement by the Other within feminism needs to be addressed by post-structuralism. Within the parameters of its own logic, it is inadequate for such feminists to be defined as conservative. As Bannerji (1993) states:

> The presence and representation of non-white women moves from the margin to the centre only to be marginalized again. Boxed into an alien

agenda in a feminist text as a variation on the theme 'woman', even when non-white women express themselves, an effect of alienation sets in with the very act itself.

(Bannerji 1993: xiii)

While there may exist a myriad of interpretations of the issue of identification, it is clear that, for the subaltern, it remains an issue. This grows out of the specificity of their experience, not in any historically linear sense; that is, not because non-racialized women, for example, have relatively less need to engage with these issues because they are past them, but because the experience of racialization along with factors such as patriarchy alter the conditions and therefore the questions and potential answers which arise out of these.

Speaking of intellectual work which arises out of the Canadian context, where minority women are engaging with theorizations of their (in)visibility, Bannerji (1993) makes the point that it is not simply a matter of seeking to have the margins represented in the liberal sense of the political endeavour. Rather she refers to the need for re-presentation, as a means whereby marginal experiences can provide insights into the entire society's organization and therefore a stepping-off point for any transformative enterprise. Here, the intention is to use this sense of re-presentation in relation to minority girls and the enterprise of elucidating a potentially transformative experience of schooling.

There are two points which require clarification in relation to this task. First, there is a difference between the position adopted by Bannerji (discussed above) and one which argues that racialized women have no Other to oppress and that this provides them with a privileged standpoint (hooks 1984). Such a position simply inverts hierarchical understandings by claiming that such compounded disadvantage is somehow epistemologically privileged. Arguing that hierarchies do not exist in this way is not the same as suggesting power differentials do not exist. Instead, it is an argument that power is played out through the micro-politics of specific interactions, responsive to particular contexts and that these interactions create and position various subject locations. Within this complex myriad of positionings, some interactions can provide insights relevant to broader issues of transformation.

Second, it is important, in this context, to reiterate Spivak's (1993) notion of deconstructing that which we hold dear. We may hold dear a social location constructed as particularly oppressed because it provides a sense of moral if not epistemological privilege. In the business of transformation, oppressive locations have a particular currency. We need to reflect on this issue of currency and its potential to interrupt anti-hegemonic articulations (Laclau and Mouffe 1985).

## Working with students and the politics of truth

I have argued that work with students may provide an alternative set of meanings to those evident through related education policies and that this may serve to unsettle common understandings and representations of ethnic minority girls. In many ways this possibility is linked to our understandings of how knowledge is produced. The studies I have described in the preceding chapters are invariably my stories. These are related to what I saw in schools and what I considered important in the words, written and spoken, of students who, in turn, responded through their understandings of what I was asking and what I wanted to hear. Without the pretence of objectivity can research tell us anything new or does it tell us only what we want to understand? This is a vexed question and feminist researchers working in education, like others, have considered the tensions and contradictions within this location.

Reflecting on her own work, Yates (1998) argues that there are two critical issues for researchers:

> the ethics and effects of the researchers' interactions with those they study . . . The other is the problem of analytic stance: a problem that traditional (and indeed any) categories of analysis and interpretation (of gender, for example; or class) create a dominant story that marginalizes some experiences; but, on the other hand, that without some analytic tools that point to some commonalities in process, we can be left with an approach that is simply self-indulgent.
>
> (Yates 1998: 3)

What are 'some commonalities in process' which can be drawn from two studies undertaken over a ten-year period, in different ways and within divergent theoretical frameworks? The aim through both of these studies has been to challenge the meanings associated with gender and ethnicity as these are presented to us through prevailing discourses. It is through the presentation of an alternative set of meanings that this is attempted. The alternative set of meanings presented here are no more (and I would claim, no less) 'real' than those that underpin the discourses they seek to challenge. There is no claim here, that the students who participated had the same definitions of racism, for example, and that comparisons can be made between some groups of students or some schools, relative to others. Similarly, there is no claim that my presence, let alone my interpretations of what constituted meaning, was not in itself a significant factor in shaping such meanings. The aim is to provide illustration of the complexity and contingent nature of gender and ethnicity within schooling, and in so doing, challenge some of the prevailing configurations, so that new meanings may be created through such contestation.

The methodologies for these studies varied. In the case of the Educating Voula study, I worked as a 'teacher' within several Victorian State secondary schools. I undertook a teaching load and was responsible for developing curriculum, teaching this and assessing students over a period of two years. The schools chosen were in lower socio-economic areas with high percentages of ethnic minority students. The classes were constructed as single sex. However, the ethnic composition of these classes responded to the categorization common at the time, that is, 'non-English-speaking background' and 'English-speaking background'. The schools selected provided a range of ethnic diversity within these categories, most commonly Greek, Italian, Turkish, Lebanese, Serbian and Croatian, constituted as the former category, and mainstream Australians and some born in the UK, constituted as the latter category.

The Bureau Study proceeded on a different premise. The commissioning body referred to 'immigrant background youth' and through the quantitative phase of the study it was intended to isolate students born in Australia and overseas-born students from particular ethnic backgrounds. This task was problematic, particularly for those born in Australia. Commonly, attempts to capture the so-called second-generation migrants through such statistical data is done through noting the language spoken at home. This tends to reflect language maintenance rather than ethnic background. In some instances, language spoken at home may refer to a range of ethnicities, as is the case for those who speak Spanish, for example. Notwithstanding these difficulties, ten groups were isolated for the qualitative phase of the study. These were Greek, Italian, Turkish, British-born, South African, Russian, Vietnamese, Chinese, Polish and El Salvadorean. Schools with relatively high enrolments of students from these groups were chosen and single-sex, ethno-specific focus groups of students were created for one-off sessions. As a result of this emphasis, the schools selected included state, private and ethno-religious secondary schools.

Through work at the school level, it was hoped to capture the subtleties behind the labels used on national databases. Students from each school were asked to self-identify with the nominated ethnic groups. It is difficult to know on what basis each did so. For many students the labels are clearly problematic. For example, some students designated themselves within the 'English' category because they were born in the UK, but were in fact ethnically Indian. Similarly, students who in some way identified with the label 'Russian' were Jewish and had vexed and ambivalent relations with this label. The Chinese label attracted a range of students from Taiwan, Hong Kong and China. Was their initial identification with the labels offered based on an understanding that nationality coincided with ethnicity? Was it based on language/s spoken? Was it determined by their interpretation of the dominant discourses and their understanding of how they were commonly defined by these? A clear limitation of the methodology adopted was the predetermination of the categories offered to students on the basis of externally and bureaucratically defined criteria for concepts as complex as ethnicity.

## Naming and thus creating

Chapter 2 provided some background into ways in which cultural difference has been represented within Australia. Such difference exists to a great extent through the categories we use to name it. Much has been written about the use of labels and the ways in which such labelling creates and consolidates certain groups as 'other'. In the Australian context, categories such as 'migrant', 'second- and third-generation migrant', 'non-English-speaking background', 'immigrant background', 'new Australian', 'ethnic minority' and 'Asian' are some labels used to denote difference from 'Australian' (Castles *et al.* 1988; Pettman 1992; Gunew and Yeatman 1993; Vasta and Castles 1996; Hage 1998). I am mindful of the ways in which my adoption of such categories maintains this division. Despite this I persist with the categories 'ethnic minority' and 'ethnic majority' or 'mainstream'. These categories reflect the difference between those imagined as 'real Australians' and those imagined as 'unreal Australians'. If this difference did not exist there would be little point to this exploration. Past these categories, students were attached to labels such as 'Greek', 'Italian' or 'Russian' through self-attribution.

The most important power differential between myself as researcher/author and the students and others with whom I worked is that which comes from the naming of such categories. In the first study this exercise was informed by a feminist understanding that it was possible for a researcher/author to voice a silence, particularly if there was an imagined symmetry between the researched and the researcher. This was a time when a comfortable theoretical cul-de-sac existed for the researcher who identified with libratory praxis. In line with this, my research took the form of 'teacher's work', my advocacy was related to a group with whom I identified and my academic work was worthwhile because it engaged with a change process through policy, pedagogy and the professional development of teachers. By 1994 this was no longer a theoretical 'comfort zone' given the very little kudos involved in the creation of an alternative set of essentialisms, in this case 'ethnic minority girls'. The methodology adopted for the later study makes no nods in these directions. Rather it was an attempt to use the master's tools to dismantle his own house (Lorde 1984).

In part this shift is a reflection of my inability to create a third path between 'radical' and 'mainstream' ontologies in the context of anti-essentialist feminism. How do we study a group of students without naming them as a group and in the process risking essentialism? Spivak (1993: 16) asks 'why essentialism is confused with the empirical'. In exploring this she makes the point that some anti-essentialist work is so self-consciously so, that it offers very few insights. Instead she argues a path between developing essences and ignoring the empirical. By 'knowing the limits of one's power' and understanding that one person's work is a fragment of a whole developed in response to their own 'inclinations and capacities', she argues that a broader picture may be developed. She describes this as a 'collective enterprise'. In this way she also challenges the binary opposition between the investigator and the audience, acknowledging the latter's capacity to read between the lines and take the story somewhere else (Spivak 1993: 16–17). What follows evolves out of my 'inclinations and capacities' and is offered in the spirit of Spivak's notion of collectivism. These are the themes that evolve out of the two studies previously described. For me, they represent important directions for the continued exploration of the issues at the heart of this book: that is, how do we engage with the educational dilemma related to equity and difference through a feminist politics of difference?

# 7 Equality AND difference

In Australia, much of the thinking related to educational equity and differ-ence has been earmarked by the term 'inclusive curriculum'. This has been so particularly in relation to policy and related activity within schools. There has been a debate about the type of equality encompassed through this term and its various applications to class and/or gender, for example (Yates 1987a, 1988). The foundation of inclusive curriculum has been the acknowledgement that marginalized students enter the classroom with a set of cultural understandings that do not coincide with those transferred through the curriculum. As educators we are faced with the dilemma of teaching students what is necessary for success by unteaching their culture or reinforcing their culture at the risk of failure. Educationists have engaged in various ways with this dilemma and in Victoria, much of the thinking around inclusive curriculum has related to gender equity specifically. Within these debates, marginal students have been variously constructed as 'girls' or 'working-class students' and considered in relation to the main-stream as the hegemonic. Through the schooling experiences of ethnic minority girls and the themes which arise out of the two studies previously described, I wish to consider anti-hegemonic articulations (Laclau and Mouffe 1985) and through these a feminist praxis of difference in relation to schooling. If we are to consider the relationships between anti-hegemonic movements as themselves unequal the relationship between these adds to the complexities and possibilities of a politics of difference. How do teachers understand the culture which students bring with them to the classroom? Within these understandings what is privileged and how does this impact on the schooling experiences of students? With reference to ethnic minority girls these issues are particularly pertinent given the prevalence of the culture clash analysis within both hegemonic and anti-hegemonic discourses.

## Culture and schooling

Primary in such an exploration are the understandings of culture which underpin the relevant discourses. Within policies that privilege the notion of 'culture clash', there is a view of culture as static and dichotomized, evoking the image of two distinct forces (family and school) each with its own momentum, destined to collide and crush anything hapless enough to be positioned between them (ethnic minority girls).

Such understandings are premised on imagined, fictitious or idealized notions of the particular cultures which form the Australian pastiche. There is the idealized version of the British Australia which went to war for king and country; the radically egalitarian Australia which has its origins in Irish convicts, bushranging and labour movements. There is the idealized version of the tolerant, liberal and multicultural nation taking in the poor and the war-torn and promising them opportunity through hard work. There is the romanticized version of the many minority homelands with their traditions, values and customs emerging out of centuries of history. Each of these imaginings is created, reinforced and reinterpreted through the discourses of politics, schooling, popular culture and the media as these operate within and between minority communities, mainstream society and the homelands of diasporic communities.

The view of minority and majority cultures as separate in this way has been challenged and instead there is an effort to concentrate on the interdependencies and fluidity of culture and identity. In relation to schooling specifically, particular attention has been given to the role of popular culture as a means whereby students interpret complex cultural identifications (McCarthy and Crichlow 1990). For me, the issues which are thrown into stark relief by Australian students' descriptions of their experiences, are best illuminated by the concept of diasporization, that is, a view of identities as 'irrevocably the product of several interlocking histories and cultures' (Hall 1996b).

Hall (1996b) argues that diasporic identities are those situated in-between different cultures. This location allows them to unsettle the assumptions of one culture from the perspective of another. In this way, diasporic communities are understood not as stranded minorities, but as providing, through the lived experiences of their members, insights into cultural production as it occurs in both of the locations they function between.

## Diasporization

I was a novelty, something different in the small village of Peloponiso. The first week the children of the village would crowd around me and offer lollies and rides on their animals. I was very honoured. One thing

I could not understand, however, was that they had nicknamed me the 'Australian'. Until that moment I had considered myself only a Greek. I thought it was strange, because like them I had a Greek background, Greek parents, and followed Greek traditions.

This piece was written by a Year 12 girl who participated in the Educating Voula study. For many, the first trip 'home' is a means of recognizing that their cultural identifications are as much to do with the way they see themselves as they are a product of how others see them. Similarly, they recognize that their difference from both their 'home' culture and Australian culture produces something new which is a product of both. In students' comments are indications that they do not always live their lives or project their futures in terms compatible with an understanding of culture as static and dichotomized between crisply delineated boundaries. While these boundaries are understood, they are not necessarily accepted *per se* but instead form the backdrop for a range of complex cultural negotiations which are framed by context and in this way are contingent in response to a given specificity. That many Australians, and indeed people all over the world, are linked irrevocably with multiple histories and cultures is clear. Also clear is that this is seen by many as ongoing and positive. Many Australians are highlighting these complexities through literature which describes new Australian identities and cultures (Gunew and Longley 1992; Pallotta-Chiarolli 1999). How we understand the experience of living with such cultural complexities is significant in terms of the schooling experience we help frame as educationists. Do we understand 'interlocking histories and cultures' in positive ways or in ways which indicate incomplete or unsuccessful assimilation, or resistance to assimilation?

## Diasporic solutions

The groups interviewed through the Educating Voula and Bureau Studies were diverse and (as has already been outlined) represented groups with various lengths of residency in Australia. Similarly, their academic achievement was varied. What is more, no direct link could be argued between this length of residency and academic achievement. Instead, however, a link could be argued tentatively, between groups with high academic involvement and achievement and an historic diasporic experience.

While the notion of the diaspora has existed for many hundreds of years, there is a clear and recognized need to consider it afresh in the context of globalization. Instead of considering minority groups as constituting outposts of one nation-state within another nation-state, diasporas are increasingly posited as groups with experience in global cultural production, political and economic concerns which make them well placed to take advantage of the new era. Cohen (1997) argues that diasporic communities have a range of skills among which he includes entrepreneurship, the building and utilization of networks and a facility with education. While Cohen refuses to homogenize the diasporic experience, he none the less makes the point worthy of attention in this context that they are marked by 'a passion for knowledge' which contributes to upward mobility. He is adamant, however, that success cannot be understood through 'economic-speak' but instead through the interrelationship between the economic and the cultural. He states:

> as it is with business ventures, so it is with the market place of ideas, the plastic and performing arts, literary endeavours and other forms of cultural production . . . diasporas score by being able to interrogate the universal with the particular and by being able to use their cosmopolitanism to press the limits of the local.
>
> (Cohen 1997: 173)

Diasporic communities in this sense may or may not be immigrant communities. One distinguishing feature is an ongoing relationship with their country of origin and through this their links with members of the same community who may reside in a range of countries. While such communities have quite distinct histories, linked in some cases with persecution and in others with expansion, Cohen attributes to them a 'passion for knowledge' which is often, but not solely, reflected in a desire for certification. He argues: 'Characteristically the choice of qualification coincides with the possibility of migration, forced or self-chosen' (Cohen 1997: 172).

In the Bureau Study this sense of diaspora was most evident with students who identified as Greek, Jewish and Chinese. These communities could claim an historic experience of diasporization regardless of place of birth and time of arrival in Australia. For some, multiple migration was part of their family history. In the case of the Greek students, most were born in Australia to parents who also had been born in Australia or immigrated at a young age. The overwhelming majority of Jewish students were born in either South Africa or Russia and had been in Australia for between two and five years. The Chinese students represented more diversity with some recently arrived from places such as Hong Kong, Taiwan, China or Vietnam and others having been born in Australia. Both within and between these categories there was a vast range of difference. One of the most interesting aspects of diasporas is the fact that they encapsulate both difference and sameness. Differences arising out of gender, class, ethnicity, language, birthplace, reasons for migration, within as well as between the categories, were evident with these Chinese, Jewish and Greek students. Yet, there were also clear commonalities because of real or imagined connections to a common culture and/or homeland.

It was striking through these interviews, how these students attached, as markers of their cultural identification, attitudes to education. Being Greek,

Chinese or Jewish meant having 'serious' attitudes towards education. Interviews with these students indicated that most were proud of the academic expectations they understood as part of their backgrounds. While this 'serious' attitude to education is often attributed to immigrants, the argument being made here, following Cohen (1997), is that in the case of diasporic groups, immigrant or otherwise, this attitude exists and is nuanced differently. It was striking through the interviews, how students from these communities had a clear sense of who they were and the relationship between this and their academic aspirations, to the extent that one Year 10 boy saw a loss of 'Greekness' as an academic disadvantage as follows:

> It all depends on the way that you have been brought up. It comes from the pressure you get from your parents. Bill's parents are more Greek. My father is more assimilated. I slack off, I think that it won't help. Greek students who still have their ethnic parents work harder. Their parents are stricter and make sure that they take school seriously.

It is worthwhile noting in this context that students from these groups described specific forms of youth culture embedded within their minority cultures. This was most obvious with the Greek and Jewish students. Within the Greek-Australian community, specific forms of youth culture are evident through its weekly newspapers, some of which include an English language supplement. An array of social venues and activities earmarked for youth, as well as a range of national and transnational organizations intended as diasporic youth forums exist. Perhaps, it is the existence of such a diasporic youth culture which allows students from these groups to create a third space between academic and mainstream popular cultures, particularly at a moment when the popular in Australia, is defined so narrowly, assuming an unproblematic and hegemonic understanding of 'Australianness'.

Through the possibility of such third spaces, can students avoid being 'daggy' and 'nerdy' in contradistinction to being academic? This issue sits at the heart of culture and schooling, influencing and being influenced by relationships between popular youth culture, the youth cultures of the school yard, definitions of the academic within and between these cultures and all of these as they are inflected by ethnicity and gender.

The students from these diasporic communities described alternative forms of youth culture which were embedded within their minority cultures. This was particularly so with the Greek and Jewish students. The Jewish students from South Africa and Russia, the Chinese and the Greek students who participated in this study, despite the significant variation which existed within each group, had in common strong, ethno-religious, community-based, cultural identifications. Students within these groups described, in straightforward ways, their identification with their respective communities.

Significant variation between and within these groups existed. In the case of the Jewish students, for example, these were marked between the South

Africans and the Russians as discussed previously. Similarly, the differences between the Chinese students were vast. None the less, these students remained, in their terms, Jewish, Chinese or Greek. They attached to each of these terms a range of cultural practices – a language (Hebrew in the case of the often multilingual Jewish students), Judaism and Greek Orthodoxy, and a community. They described a social life intrinsic to that community, in which they and their friends were happy to participate. The situations in which they socialized were not always ones formally attached to community-based organizations. In the case of one group of Greek students, for example, they described a neighbourhood tavern which had become a meeting place for them. What they enjoyed was the Greek music, way of socializing and the fact that they could share this with friends who understood the 'way we do things'. In relation to their schooling, the overwhelming majority of the Russian and South African students involved in this study attended Jewish schools and stated this was their preferred option. The Greek and Chinese students, on the other hand, attended state schools. In the case of one group of Greek students who attended a state school with a significant proportion of Greek students and a Greek language programme, they stated that this was a distinct advantage of this particular school. Many of the Greek and Chinese students also attended community-based after-hours schools. Within Greek after-hours schools, students learnt language and aspects of Greek culture, including dance, religion and history. The Chinese students who attended after-hours schools described how they were provided with Chinese language and assistance with subjects such as maths in Chinese.

I wish to pay particular attention to the gendered nature of such spaces. There are two reasons for this. First, there is the argument put forward by Hall (1996a) that in relation to anti-hegemonic spaces, there is the potential for these to reflect and consolidate traditional distributions of power related to factors such as gender, class and sexuality. Second, there is the argument that I have been developing, related to the role of gender relations in the creation of cultural boundaries, and by implication their dismantling, in the context of schooling. These issues are central to the creation of a feminist praxis of difference. The challenge is twofold: to challenge those hegemonic representations which subordinate, as well as to consider gendered power relations within third spaces as these spaces are created. I would argue that it is these challenges which are at the heart of a transformative schooling, one which does not fall into the trap of accepting difference and equity as a binary opposition.

## Gendering third spaces

Comments made by students, particularly those involved in the Educating Voula study, confirmed the important role that gender plays in the creation of boundaries between ethnic groups. Students, staff and parents commented on differences which they felt existed between the way gender was constructed within some minority communities and the Australian mainstream and how these differences delineated between these groups. A fundamental aspect of this delineation related to the sexual double standard and the view that it was applied in a way which created more restrictions on ethnic minority women and girls than it did on other women and girls. There was also an understanding that this difference was commonly linked to a 'mainstream equals enlightened/minority equals backward' binary. The following comments made by teachers during interviews illustrate this latter point.

> Turkish girls are the worst off because of Islam, peasant backgrounds and because they are newly arrived. Other girls are not as restricted because they are more assimilated.

> Some NESB [non-English-speaking-background] parents don't want daughters to go to university in case they get 'Australianized'. There is a pressure on them to get married, often by proxy.

Ironically, there is also criticism of parents from these communities for having overly high expectations.

> Schools should get NESB parents to understand what kids are capable of. Daughters are seen as potential doctors by parents. They need to be told their kids aren't good enough without insulting them.

For students, however, clear differences of perception on this issue existed within the 'wog' and 'Skip' categories. Of primary concern in this context is a comparison of the view presented by ethnic minority girls, relative to the policy literature previously discussed. While the culture clash model, common to this education literature, emphasizes the way that gender relations operate in the countries of origin and the inappropriateness of their transplantation to the Australian situation, ethnic minority girls considered gender relations in the context of the alienation and dislocation brought about by the migration process. The following comments by ethnic minority girls illustrate this point:

> In Turkey my cousins are more free than me because there are hardly any other nationalities living in Turkey like in Australia. So there, parents don't have to worry much but over here I'm not free because my parents are scared something might happen to me.

> My parents started not to let me out as much as they used to in Greece. I could not understand why at first, but then I realized myself that we were in a new country and we were surrounded by new people whom they did not know.

Through this shift of emphasis a stark contrast developed; that is, while the culture clash model develops the mainstream as a source of potential liberation for these girls, minority girls developed the mainstream as a source of added oppression. These girls argued that while the sexual double-standard was a constant, life in their mother-countries was less socially restrictive than in Australia. In Australia, they faced added restrictions because of a range of factors related to systemic racism, sexism and class oppression, which narrowed their social opportunities. Moreover, these girls did not draw up a 'mainstream equals enlightened/minority equals backward' binary, and instead described cultural shifts, in Australia and in their mother-countries, related to a new generation with new understandings of a range of issues, including gender relations. This was particularly evident in their comments on how they anticipated rearing their own children and living their lives in future relationships with husbands (Tsolidis 1990).

The vision that these girls had of themselves can be understood as diasporization. These girls actively chose not to assimilate, both because they liked aspects of their minority cultures and because they did not like aspects of mainstream culture as it was understood by them. A significant confirmation of these girls' diasporic identities also came from their experiences overseas. There they were not seen as Greek or Italian, for example, as they had been considered in Australia, but instead Australian. In this context also, these girls were not just responding to attributed characteristics, but were constructing for themselves diasporic cultural identities.

In relation to the students who were part of the school-based studies discussed here, it was the adolescent ethnic minority girls, in particular, who reflected upon the boundary-keeping roles associated with femineity. They described the pressures they experienced as a result of these. However, they also described the advantages. They did this in relation to their own lives and their pride in their minority cultural identifications, through their maintenance of language and cultural traditions. They also described what they considered to be restrictions on the ways in which they could socialize but added that this was symptomatic of a way of caring which was evident in their families. Their understanding of biculturalism as positive was also evident in their stated intent to rear their own children in this manner. Many of these girls stated that even if their future partners did not share their own ethnic background, their children would speak their language and attend ethnic community schools as the girls did themselves (Tsolidis 1986).

It is in this context that the role of gender in relation to cultural difference and processes of identification is so poignant and warrants further consideration. The relationship between gender and ethnicity is complex, as has been discussed previously. Yuval-Davis (1997) states:

Women especially are often required to carry this 'burden of representation', as they are constructed as the symbolic bearers of the collectivity's identity and honour, both personally and collectively.

(Yuval-Davis 1997: 45)

Comments made by these girls indicated the policing of their honour and the importance of this within their communities. Perhaps their projections about their future families needs to be considered in light of an optimism and naivety born of youth and inexperience. Yet within their comments also was a sense of belonging and an agency in the construction of their identifications as diasporic. This agency is also evident in the comments of minority women who are rearing their own children (Tsolidis 1999). Women from minority communities may not have straightforward relationships with their cultures and communities, much as they do not with the cultures of the mainstream. It is this ambivalence, which produces something new, rather than merely replicates the minority culture as it is understood to exist in the country of origin, or mimics the mainstream. As feminists, particularly feminist educators, we are left with a choice of understanding this ambivalence and acknowledging this agency, or constructing these women and girls simply as acted upon in the processes whereby cultures and identities are made and remade.

Through marriage, child-bearing and child-rearing and maintaining the family as a site where language, values, mores and traditions are transferred and reinterpreted – all considered traditional female domains – being a woman also brings with it the responsibility of creating a conduit between the private and public cultural spheres. In a country like Australia, the private is so often seen to coincide with the minority; the culture of the homeland, mother-tongue maintenance, significantly feminized terms. The public is seen to coincide with the mainstream, the majority, the dominant. At a theoretical level this schema is bankrupt because it presupposes that categories such as minority/majority, powerful/powerless, public/private, Australian/migrant are immutably dichotomous. Instead, the argument is developed here in relation to Australian ethnic minorities most specifically, that culture is dynamic, shifting and responsive to context and that by establishing a dialectical relationship between the private and the public we can also challenge a dichotimous relationship between minority and majority cultures.

## Women's work in cultural re/production

There is a need to challenge the distinction between the private and public domains and do so specifically in relation to the work that minority women undertake in creating third spaces. The schism so often created between the home and the school in traditional understandings of culture relegates women's cultural work to the private, minority, invisible sphere. The school is the public, the mainstream, the visible and potentially assimilationist sphere. New understandings of culture provide a possibility to challenge this binary and acknowledge the importance of women's cultural work. The lived realities of women, especially as mothers, with attendant responsibilities for the enculturation of the next generation into the social mores of communities, brings them face to face on a daily basis, with the possibilities of creating new cultural identifications. It is at once the strength and weakness implicit in the traditional expectation of feminity in relation to the maintenance of cultural boundaries. The role that women are expected to play and their contestation and renegotiation of this role, positions them at the very point where culture is re/produced, not in the sense of replicated, but in the sense of recreated anew. In addition to the issues of marriage partners and child-rearing *vis-à-vis* minority cultural maintenance discussed above, there are other issues of importance including dress, food and dance.

Food, most often associated with women, is frequently described as a marker for the establishment of such categories of differentiation. This is particularly so, in this context, in relation to the school yard. The school lunch composed of thick, unruly slices of crusty bread and salami, versus the symmetrical and disciplined white bread sandwiches spread thinly with Vegemite; these have become metaphors for the sensual, indulgent and 'uncivilized' in opposition to the restrained and the 'civilized' – metaphors for acceptance or rejection. Such representations and their poignant implications have been reiterated in the stories of minority Australians who recall their school days (Loh 1980; Brunswick Oral History Project 1985; Carew 1997).

The reference to food in relation to cultural difference and the acceptance of this difference through Australian multiculturalism has been justly criticized. The metaphor of the happy Australian family which is as accepting of spaghetti as it is of stir fries or curries has been decried by commentators for masking the real inequalities underpinning cultural difference and the fact that tolerance of this difference is superficial rather than engrained in Australian institutional practice (Kalantzis and Cope 1984, 1987). Still it persists through, for example, a magazine reference to 'Mediterasian' as the character of Australian cuisine.

Yet at another level, the seemingly trivial cultural baggage of food, language, dance and dress represent a possible conduit for a politics of difference. The Turkish girls who chose to make a statement through wearing both traditional Turkish and contemporary Australian clothing are one example of this possibility. For many minority students the school lunch represents a stark choice between presenting or hiding the private in the public space of the school yard. In this way, this often-referred-to food-based expression of culture clash is still somewhat profound. Along similar lines, there is the recognition that within bilingual families, children as young as 3 resist speaking their mother-tongue in public even though they may speak it at home. Such issues of food, language and dress are played out within the traditional female domains related to the kitchen, the crèche, the school lunch box and the 'soft' aspects of communities. So often, such issues become the mechanisms for contested and evolving self-imaging. Rather than always trivial, such issues can be conduits for a politics of resistance against racism through the creation of unassimilated and interlocking identifications.

As feminist educators, our attitudes to such issues are framed by the position we adopt *vis-à-vis* difference and equity. Perhaps some school-based examples will illustrate my point. At one school with which I was involved during the studies, there was ongoing debate regarding swimming classes and the participation of Muslim girls who were not prepared to attend such activities if these were coeducational. One response was to ignore these girls who were consequently left with non-participation as their only option. This position was underpinned by a toothless pluralism which did not challenge normative configurations of gender and cultural relations. The alternative position adopted was one that argued equality on the assumption that this meant sameness. It was assumed that the girls wished to participate on the terms provided and that their families had prohibited them from doing so. In this context, families were confronted and accused of denying their daughters full participation. Again, this option most often led to non-participation. Eventually a third way was developed. Some teachers organized female-only sessions at the baths in which girls who wanted single-sex participation could attend.

Similarly in some schools there was concern about minority girls' participation in sport, more generally. It was assumed that ethnic minority girls avoided participation in sport for reasons related to gender roles within their cultures. Commonly, the sports offered included Australian rules football, traditionally a male domain, and sports such as hockey, softball and netball, understood as more 'girl friendly'. In some schools, with large numbers of minority students, soccer was offered, a sport commonly associated with ethnic minorities in Australia. Within some schools, there existed a segregation with girls, including minority girls, doing traditional girls' sports. In other schools, girls were encouraged into the full range of sports offered, including those deemed male. In such situations, ethnic minority girls were encouraged to play soccer. If we consider Scott's (1990) argument about difference and equity, this an example of gender equity understood as sameness or difference, as difference from the male. However, through this example, I wish to illustrate how such dynamics normalize cultural difference and through this compound the subordination of minority girls. In the segregated approach, 'girl friendly' is understood in mainstream cultural terms through the offering of sports such as hockey and netball. In the alternative approach, minority is taken to be male, through the investment in soccer. Some schools created a third way by broadening definitions of sport, past the traditional hockey, softball, football and soccer, into areas such as gymnastics, dance (traditional and other) and aerobics, activities which are varied and have a potentially wider cultural base – activities in which many ethnic minority girls were involved outside school.

In such cases, the critical question for me is not the activities within which girls should participate, the critical aspect is the agency attributed to girls and the role we envisage for ourselves as educators in relation to this agency. If we assume no agency on the part of the girls themselves and see ourselves as advocates for these girls, we are accepting a framework which accepts and consolidates an empowered/disempowered binary (Ellsworth 1992; Gore 1992). While this is a familiar debate within feminist pedagogy, it is rarely ethnicized. Differences between girls remain an invisible issue and because of this, existing power differentials as these operate across and within ethnic and gender boundaries remain uncontested. In order to explore this issue I shall return more directly to the questions described in the introductory chapter as central to this exploration. How can we understand, with the assistance of feminist theorizations, equity and difference within education as other than an oppositional binary?

The aim of exploring a feminist praxis of difference is shaped by the optimism that feminist theorizations of difference have much to offer educationists in working through the equity/difference dilemma. The relationship between equity and difference has been fertile ground for feminist consideration. Increasingly, this relationship has been explored as it applies to differences between women, as well as differences between women and men. Intrinsic to this debate has been the traditional association between equity and a politics of change premised on identity politics. In Chapter 3 this was considered in relation to education policies related to gender equity and these were contrasted with multicultural policies which advocated a pluralism, which in terms of equity offered very little. I now wish to consider the argument, that rather than take sides between equity and difference, the task is to challenge the construction of these concepts as oppositional.

In her discussion of difference and equity, Scott (1990) frames her argument in relation to feminist strategy and instances where women are squeezed into a framework which offers a choice between arguing equality with men, taken to mean sameness, or difference from men, taken to be inequality. The context for her argument is women's work. She states:

> Placing equality and difference in antithetical relationship has, then, a double effect. It denies the way in which difference has long figured in political notions of equality and it suggest that sameness is the only ground on which equality can be claimed. It thus puts feminists in an impossible position, for as long as we argue within the terms of a discourse set up by this opposition we grant the current conservative premise that because women cannot be identical to men in all respects, we cannot expect to be equal to them.
>
> (Scott 1990: 144)

Scott advocates a two-step strategy. First, an insistence on difference, but in ways which challenge normative constructions of it. These, she argues, commonly construct difference as either a 'happy pluralism' or bounded by hierarchies which are accepted as 'truths'. Her second step is to insist on equality premised on differences: 'differences that confound, disrupt, and render ambiguous the meaning of any fixed binary opposition' (Scott 1990: 144).

While Scott is concerned with difference between women and men, her argument has clear relevance to differences among women. In fact it is the differences among women (and men) which strengthen her argument about the differences between women and men. Challenging the normative constructions of cultural differences, it seems to me, is one way to 'confound, disrupt, and render ambiguous the meaning of any fixed binary opposition' (Scott 1990: 144).

Many feminists are considering ways whereby a politics can be created which maintains a meaningful engagment with difference (Young 1990, 1997; Benhabib *et al.* 1995). In their discussion of the need to dismantle these concepts as oppositional, Gunew and Yeatman (1993) state:

> the major concern is to shift debates beyond the current preoccupation with binary oppositions that invariably absorbs altereity into the hegemonic and familiar. Whenever such thinking prevails, we are merely in the business of juggling with traditional categories, privileging women rather than men, or some women at the expense of others, without changing the power structures behind such constructions.
>
> (Gunew and Yeatman 1993: xiii)

It is in this spirit that I have sought to develop themes from the studies that have the potential to draw us out of the impasse and assist us to consider a politics of difference within schooling.

In this book I have made several interlocking arguments. I have referred to the various feminist theorizations of difference and their application to a politics of change, as the possibility of being feminist and being different. This feminist praxis of difference, I argue, is a significant tool for educationists in dismantling equality and difference as oppositional constructs. The schooling experiences of Australian ethnic minority students, most particularly girls, have been used to illustrate the existence and shortcomings of approaches which construct equality and difference as binary oppositions. I have also argued that such binary constructions are underpinned by an understanding of culture as static, bounded and essential. Through the students' narratives I have argued that culture is, instead, dynamic, contingent and fluid. Schooling, particularly during adolescence, is a significant cultural context and that through it, students are offered opportunities to learn, experiment, reinterpret and determine identifications. Gender and ethnicity are pivotal for these students in such processes. Contrary to the common understanding of culture clash which positions minority students, most particularly girls, as victims of irreconcilable differences, I have argued that these girls are precariously positioned at the point where cultures are remade.

Women are most often expected to enculturate the next generation. I have argued that implicit in this location are both strengths and weaknesses. At one level it represents the expectation that women will continue the culture of the fathers and is testimony to the oppression they experience. At another level, it is a location that is at the cutting edge of cultural identifications and for minority women, diasporic identifications. It is through this location that women contest, negotiate and reinterpret new cultural understandings. In this way 'women's work' forms the crux of a dialectical process whereby diasporization occurs. In order to appreciate this location as one with such a dialectical potential, the women and girls who occupy it have to be granted subjectivity and agency. Through the representations of southern European women in Australian society and through the understanding of these women's and their daughters' location within reformist education policy concerned with gender equity or multiculturalism, I have argued that such subjectivity and agency are rarely if ever granted in both reactionary and progressive discourses. Instead, the invisibility of these women and girls, or the construction of them in deficit terms, creates a social and educational context, which makes their location precarious rather than powerful.

Racism is a powerful force and, as one mother argued during an interview, mainstream understandings of minority cultures as exceptionally patriarchal are 'part of the repertoire of racism, a comment used to keep migrants down'. Feminists have to understand the potential of feminism to reinscribe racism. In Spivak's (1993) terms we have to deconstruct the labels we hold dear as well as the labels we seek to challenge. In schools, this requires teachers to contemplate anew the cultural identifications that surround them through their students. Teachers have an obligation to assist in the construction of schools as spaces which allow students to contest, negotiate and recreate cultural identifications. We should not expect these cultural identifications to be familiar to us. Indeed if they were familiar, they would not be new.

# Appendix 1:
## The 1984 Educating Voula study

The methodology for this school-based study had three key elements. First, the shared sex and ethnic status of the author and the subject group were understood as a foundation of the methodology; second, the decision was taken to establish classes of ethnic minority girls rather than discussion groups; third, the work done with these classes provided the basis for subsequent work carried out with discussion groups of ethnic minority boys and ethnic majority girls and boys. The school-based study had five elements.

### Work with ethnic minority girls

This work took the form of classes made up only of ethnic minority girls. These classes were long-term and operated as an integrated part of the existing school timetables. Seven core groups of ethnic minority girls were included in the study.

In addition, there were three non-core groups: one group who were part of a pilot study and two groups of Year 12 ethnic minority studying their mother-tongues. These classes operated in 1985 and 1986 respectively, and centred on bilingual writings on themes related to being an ethnic minority girl living in Australia. These girls' writing was published by the Victorian Ministry of Education under the title *In Our Own Words* (MACMME undated).

Although each class dealt with the same issues, the way this was done varied in relation to the year level and the subject in which the study was embedded. The work undertaken in these classes addressed ethnic minority girls' academic and vocational aspirations and their views on cultural identification.

Features common to these classes were as follows:

- no class was made up of only one ethnic group
- all classes covered the same topics

- the girls were assessed by the author for the work they did in these classes in line with each school assessment procedures
- girls were given the opportunity to dissent if they did not wish to participate in these classes
- all the participants were told that the class was part of a study and the aims of the study were explained
- the girls were asked to evaluate these classes.

## Work with the other groups of students

The work carried out with these groups of students did not take the same form as that undertaken by the ethnic minority girls. Instead of long-term classes being established, a series of focus group sessions were organized in which the students worked on and discussed a number of worksheets. The worksheets were based on the work undertaken with the ethnic minority girls. These students were asked to work individually to complete each worksheet and then participate in a whole-group discussion on the issues raised.

## Formal interviews conducted with staff and parents

A number of staff in each of the three schools were interviewed and their selection was based on a range of considerations. An attempt was made to include both males and females, ethnic minority and ethnic majority staff, a range of curriculum areas and positions of responsibility, as well as a range of attitudes to the sorts of issues that were being canvassed. These interviews were conducted on a one-to-one basis with all staff responding to the same questions. Additionally, numbers of parents from each school were interviewed. These was undertaken either as intensive interviews with one parent or through the establishment of ethno-specific focus groups. Table 1 provides details related to the students who participated in this study.

Terms used to describe ethnicity in this context were those used by the students to describe their own backgrounds. All parents of ethnic minority students were born overseas.

Of the twenty-five ethnic majority girls who participated in this study, one was born outside Australia (Ireland). Their parents (numbering 50) were mostly born in Australia; however, of the total number of 50 parents six were born in England, three in Ireland and two in Scotland. Overseas-born parents were often married to Australia-born partners.

Similarly, with the twenty-six ethnic majority boys, only one was born overseas (England); three parents were born in England and one in Scotland.

*Table 1*  Student participants in the Educating Voula study

| Ethnicity | Number | Australian-born | Overseas-born |
|---|---|---|---|
| *Girls* | | | |
| Greek | 25 | 23 | 2 |
| Turkish | 22 | 3 | 19 |
| Yugoslav | 13 | 13 | |
| Italian | 6 | 6 | |
| Lebanese | 5 | 1 | 4 |
| Maltese | 5 | 5 | |
| Macedonian | 3 | 2 | 1 |
| Spanish | 1 | 1 | |
| Hungarian | 1 | 1 | |
| Albanian | 1 | 1 | |
| Polish/Yugoslav | 1 | 1 | |
| French/Yugoslav | 1 | 1 | |
| Portuguese | 1 | | 1 |
| Chilean | 1 | | 1 |
| | | | |
| *Boys* | | | |
| Greek | 17 | 16 | 1 |
| Turkish | 8 | 1 | 7 |
| Yugoslav | 6 | | 6 |
| Italian | 2 | 2 | |
| Macedonian | 1 | 1 | |
| Maltese | 1 | | 1 |
| Lebanese | 1 | | 1 |
| Syrian | 1 | 1 | |
| Cypriot | 1 | | 1 |

# Appendix 2:
# The 1994 Bureau study

The focus within this study was the educational achievements of targeted groups within the 15–24 cohort of Australians. The aim was to identify potential birthplace, ethnic and gender differences in key aspects of educational access and attainment, experience and aspirations.

## Access and attainment

A broad mapping of existing statistical data was undertaken at the national level to determine educational reality as it correlated with migrancy, ethnic background and gender. This was undertaken in relation to upper post-primary education and the fullest range of tertiary provision. Within the university sector, this analysis extended to fields of study and course type.

## Experience and aspirations

Educational experience and aspirations and how these may inhibit or facilitate educational attainment was examined through case-study work with particular communities. In the selection of these particular communities, attention has been paid to a range of factors including length of residency in Australia, visibility within the community, commonsense understandings related to particular ethnic groups' migration experience, demographic factors and patterns which had emerged from the quantitative research. This work was undertaken with upper post-primary students in Melbourne and Brisbane. Supplementary material was gathered from focus group discussions with parents from the relevant communities and teachers.

## Quantitative research

The quantitative research was achieved primarily through analysis of data from sources including Australian Bureau of Statistics (ABS) 1991 Census material and Department of Education, Employment and Training (DEET) data including that for 1993.

### ABS 1991 census

The 1991 Census data were used to answer quesions relating to the educational access and attainment of 15- to 24-year-olds residing in Australia. The Census data contain responses to the following questions on highest education attainment (HEA), age, gender, ethnicity, birthplace, years in Australia and family income. Subdividing the data to these levels means it is possible to get below the aggregated level of 'immigrant' performance to consider educational access and attainment of subgroups and thus identify those who are significantly under-represented.

A major consideration was to identify associations between certain factors in relation to HEA including:

- birthplace, ethnicity and HEA
- family income, ethnicity, birthplace and HEA
- years in Australia, ethnicity and HEA
- gender, ethnicity, birthplace and HEA.

### DEET data

From the data supplied by DEET, students of immigrant backgrounds can be identified according to their country of birth, year of arrival in Australia and language spoken at home. Using these data higher education enrolments are analysed in relation to birthplace, ethnicity and gender. This analysis identified differences in enrolments by course type and field of study in relation to factors such as birthplace, ethnicity and gender. This allowed consideration of whether specific groups of students were over- or under-represented in certain fields of study and at particular institutions.

## Qualitative research

### Students

While the quantitative research provided an overall mapping of educational access and attainments, the qualitative aspects of the study provided insights into the educational experience at the school level and the ways in which it facilitated or hindered this.

The qualitative research concentrated on upper post-primary students in order to investigate their educational aspirations and experiences. For reasons of costs, the qualitative research was undertaken in Brisbane and Melbourne only.

Single-sex groups of approximately six to ten students mostly from Year 11 were formed in a range of schools. Priority was given to ethnic identification and this became the primary basis for the selection of the schools involved in the study. In order to determine which schools had students from the targeted ethnic groupings enrolled, Education Department data were used, as well as a widely distributed invitation to participate. Where possible, a range of provision – including state, independent, Catholic and single sex – was included. Similarly, consideration was given to geographic and socio-economic variation where possible.

Students were asked to complete a questionnaire, after which a group discussion was conducted. In this way, both immediate and individual responses, as well as those shaped through discussion, were included.

Single-sex groups were organized to facilitate the recognition of gender differentiated responses and to ensure that girls would have the opportunity to respond fully and freely during the interviews.

In Melbourne these sessions were conducted by members of the research team with teaching qualifications and experience. In Brisbane, a team of practising teachers was established and briefed by the researchers through teleconferencing. The interview sessions were conducted as classes with questions explained, time-frames established for completion of the questionnaires, emphasis given to private written responses, eliciting frank and full answers and orderliness of spoken responses during discussion. In this context, preference was given to teaching experience rather than research experience when selecting personnel for the school-based work in Brisbane. Where necessary interpreters were used.

## Staff

Focus groups of teachers were established in Melbourne and Brisbane. These groups were conducted in a similar fashion to those with students, except they were not single sex. Participants were asked to complete a questionnaire based on the one the students were asked to complete. Similarly, they were interviewed after the completion of this questionnaire.

In Brisbane, this activity was organized as a workshop at a state professional development conference for ESL teachers. It was listed as one of a range of elected workshops for participants with the aims explicitly stated. Initially, close to twenty teachers indicated an interest in the workshop; however, on the day the numbers fell significantly. As a result of this, and because of the difficulties involved for the Melbourne-based researchers to travel to Brisbane, the number of teachers interviewed there was small.

*Table 2*  Student participants in the Bureau Study

| Ethnicity | Number | Australian-born | Overseas-born |
|---|---|---|---|
| *Girls* | | | |
| Chinese | 29 | | 29 |
| Vietnamese | 29 | 29 | |
| Italian | 23 | 23 | |
| Greek | 22 | 22 | |
| Russian | 15 | | 15 |
| South African | 13 | 13 | |
| Polish | 12 | | 12 |
| Turkish | 11 | 6 | 5 |
| El Salvadorean | 7 | 1 | 6 |
| British | 5 | 1 | 4 |
| *Boys* | | | |
| Italian | 27 | 27 | |
| Chinese | 25 | | 25 |
| Vietnamese | 21 | 21 | |
| Greek | 13 | 13 | |
| Russian | 13 | | 13 |
| South African | 12 | | 12 |
| Turkish | 12 | 10 | 2 |
| Polish | 10 | | 10 |
| El Salvadorean | 9 | 9 | |
| British | 7 | 7 | |

Table 2 provides details related to the students involved in the 1994 Bureau Study.

It is important to note that while the intention was to interview those born in the UK as a means of capturing the experiences of a migrant group with assumed relatively compatible cultural and linguistic attributes to those of the mainstream, this proved very difficult. In some cases those born in the UK were ethnically distinct, in others students born in Australia but whose parents were born in the UK identified strongly with Irish, Scottish or English culture and self-selected for this category.

# Bibliography

Abu Duhou, I. and Teese, R. (1992) *Education, Work Force and Community Participation of Arab Australians: Egyptians, Lebanese, Palestinians and Syrians.* Canberra: Australian Government Publishing Service for the Office of Multicultural Affairs.

Al Anwar (1989) Why Arab students fail in Australia, *An-Nahar*, 27 April.

Alcorso, C. and Schofield, T. (1991) *National Non-English Speaking Background Women's Health Strategy.* Canberra: Australian Government Publishing Service.

Anthias, F. and Yuval-Davis, N. (1983) Contextualizing feminism: gender, ethnic and class divisions, *Feminist Review*, 15: 62–75.

Anthias, F. and Yuval-Davis, N. (1992) *Racialized Boundaries: Race, Nation, Gender, Colour and Class and the Anti-racist Struggle.* London and New York: Routledge.

Anzaldua, G. (1987) *Borderlands/La Frontera: The New Mestiza.* San Francisco, CA: Spinsters/Aunt Lute.

Arnot, M. David, M. and Weiner, G. (1998) *Closing the Gender Gap: Postwar Education and Social Change.* Cambridge: Polity Press.

Athanasou, C. (995) *Hybrids: Stories of Greek Australia.* Rose Bay, NSW: Brandl and Schlesinger.

Attwood, B. (ed.) (1996) *In the Age of Mabo: History, Aborigines and Australia.* St Leonards, NSW: Allen & Unwin.

Australian Education Council (1993) *National Action Plan for the Education of Girls 1993–1997.* Carlton, Victoria: Curriculum Corporation and Australian Education Council.

Bannerji, H. (ed.) (1993) *Returning the Gaze: Essays on Racism, Feminism and Politics.* Toronto: Sister Vision.

Barrett, M. and McIntosh, M. (1985) Ethnocentrism and socialist-feminist theory, *Feminist Review*, 20: 23–47.

Bauman, Z. (1997) *Postmodernity and its Discontents.* New York: New York University Press.

Benhabib, S., Butler, J., Cornell, D., Fraser, N. and Nicholson, L. (1995) *Feminist Contentions: A Philosophical Exchange.* New York and London: Routledge.

Bhaba, H. (1983) The other question: the stereotype and colonial discourse, *Screen*, 24(6): 18–36.

Bird Rose, D. (1996) Histories and rituals: land claims in the Territory, in B. Attwood (ed.) *In the Age of Mabo: History, Aborigines and Australia*. St Leonards, NSW: Allen & Unwin.

Birrell, B. and Khoo, S. (1995) *The Second Generation in Australia: Educational and Occupational Characteristics*. Canberra: Bureau of Immigration, Multicultural and Population Research/Australia Government Publishing Scheme.

Birrell, B. and Seitz, A. (1986) The myth of ethnic inequality in Australian education, *Journal of the Australian Population Association*, 3(1): 52–74.

Birrell, B., Dobson, I., Rapson, V. and Smith, T.F. (1995) Female achievement in higher education and the professions, *People and Place*, 3(1): 43–54.

Blaikie, G. (1979) *Great Australian Scandals*. Adelaide: Rigby.

Blainey, G. (1984) *All for Australia*. Sydney: Methuen Haynes.

Bligh, V. (1983) A study of the needs of Aboriginal women who have been raped or sexually assaulted, in F. Gale (ed.) *We Are Bosses Ourselves*. Canberra: Australian Institute of Aboriginal Studies.

Bottomley, G. (1984) Women on the move: migration and feminism, in G. Bottomley and M. de Lepervanche (eds) *Ethnicity, Class and Gender in Australia*. Sydney: Allen & Unwin.

Bottomley, G. (1992) *From Another Place: Migration and the Politics of Culture*. Cambridge: Cambridge University Press.

Bottomley, G., de Lepervanche, M. and Martin, J. (eds) (1991) *Intersexions: Gender/Class/Culture/Ethnicity*. Sydney: Allen & Unwin.

Boyle, H. (1983) The conflicting role of Aboriginal women in today's society, in F. Gale (ed.) *We Are Bosses Ourselves*. Canberra: Australian Institute of Aboriginal Studies.

Brah, A. (1996) *Cartographies of Diaspora: Contesting Identities*. London and New York: Routledge.

Branson, J. and Miller, D. (1979) *Class, Sex and Education in Capitalist Society*. Malvern, Vic.: Sorrett Publishing.

Brittan, A. and Maynard, M. (1984) *Sexism, Racism and Oppression*. New York: Basil Blackwell.

Brunswick Oral History Project (1985) *For a Better Life We Came . . .*, Brunswick, NJ: Brunswick City Council.

Bullivant, B. (1988) The ethnic success ethic: ubiquitous phenomenon in English speaking societies?, *Ethnic and Racial Studies*, 11(1): 63–84.

Cahill, D. and Ewen, J. (1987) *Ethnic Youth: Their Assets and Aspirations*. Canberra: Australian Government Publishing Service.

Carew, Z. (1997) *From Capers to Quandongs*. Country Idylls, PO Box 197, Salisbury, SA, 5108.

Castles, S. (1997) Multicultural citizenship: a response to the dilemma of globalisation and national identity?, *Journal of Intercultural Studies*, 18(1): 5–22.

Castles, S., Cope, M., Kalantzis, M. and Morrissey, M. (1988) *Mistaken Identity: Multiculturalism and the Demise of Nationalism in Australia*. Sydney: Pluto Press.

Cauchi, M., (1987) *Education and the Maltese in Australia*. Melbourne: Maltese Community Council of Victoria.

Chow, R. (1993) *Writing Diaspora: Tactics of Intervention in Contemporary Cultural Studies*. Bloomington, IN: Indiana University Press.

Cohen, R. (1997) *Global Diasporas: An Introduction*. Seattle, WA: University of Washington Press.

Collins, P. (1990) *Black Feminist Thought*. Boston, MA: Unwin Hyman.

Committee of Review of Post Arrival Programs and Services to Migrants (1978) *Report of the Review of Post Arrival Programs and Services to Migrants*. Canberra: Australian Government Publishing Service.

Committee on Multicultural Education (1979) *Education for a Multicultural Society*. Report to the Schools Commission, Canberra: Australian Government Publishing Service.

Commonwealth Education Portfolio Group (1979) *Commonwealth Education Portfolio Discussion Paper on Education in a Multicultural Australia*. Canberra: Australian Government Publishing Service.

Commonwealth Schools Commission (1984) *Girls and Tomorrow: The Challenge for Schools. Report of the Working Party on the Education of Girls*. Canberra: Commonwealth Schools Commission.

Commonwealth Schools Commission (1986) *The Education of Girls in Australian Schools: Interim Report*. Canberra: Commonwealth Schools Commission.

Commonwealth Schools Commission (1987) *The National Policy for the Education of Girls in Australian Schools*. Canberra: Commonwealth Schools Commission.

Connell, R. W. (1993) *Schools and Social Justice*. Toronto: Our Schools/ Our Selves Education Foundation.

Consultative Council for Health and Human Relations Education (1980) *Health and Human Relations Education in Schools*. Melbourne: Education Department of Victoria.

Cope, B. and Morrissey, M. (1986) The immigration debate: populism, neoconservatism and multiculturalism: sketches towards a thesis. Paper presented at the Australian Institute of Multicultural Affairs, Ethnicity and Multiculturalism 1986 National Research Conference, University of Melbourne, 14–16 May.

Davis, A. Y. (1981) *Women, Race and Class*. London: Women's Press.

Davis, A. Y. (1989) *Women, Culture, and Politics*. New York: Random House.

de Lauretis, T. (1990) Upping the anti (sic) in feminist theory, in M. Hirsch and E. Fox Keller (eds) *Conflicts in Feminism*. New York: Routledge.

de Lepervanche, M. (1980) From race to ethnicity, *Australian and New Zealand Journal of Sociology*, 16(1): 24–39.

de Lepervanche, M. (1988) Racism and sexism in Australian national life, in M. de Lepervanche and G. Bottomley (eds) *The Cultural Construction of Race*. Sydney Studies in Society and Culture. Sydney: University of Sydney.

de Lepervanche, M. (1989) Women, nation and the state in Australia, in N. Yuval-Davis and F. Anthias (eds) *Woman–Nation–State*. London: Macmillan.

DEET/NBEET (Department of Employment, Education and Training/National Board of Employment, Education and Training) (1990) *A Fair Chance For All: National and Institutional Planning for Equity in Higher Education. A Discussion Paper*. Canberra: Australian Government Publishing Service.

Department of Immigration and Ethnic Affairs (1986) *Don't Settle for Less: Report of the Committee for Stage 1 of the Review of Migrant and Multicultural Programs and Services*. Canberra: Australian Government Publishing Service.

Dobson, I. (1995) A fair chance for whom? Paper given at the Second National Conference on Equity and Access in Tertiary Education, Melbourne, 4–8 July.

Education Department of Victoria (undated) *Equal Opportunity and Elimination of Sexism: A Policy Statement of the Education Department of Victoria*. Melbourne.

Ellsworth, E. (1992) 'Why doesn't this feel empowering? Working through the repressive myths of critical pedagogy, in C. Luke and J. Gore (eds) *Feminisms and Critical Pedagogy*. New York: Routledge.

Faust, B. (1993) Steering a careful course for cultural recognition, *The Age* (Melbourne), 5 February.

Fine, M., Weis, L., Powell, L. and Mun Wong, L. (eds) (1997) *Off White: Readings on Race, Power, and Society*. New York and London: Routledge.

Foster, L.E. (1988) *Diversity and Multicultural Education: A Sociological Perspective*. Sydney: Allen & Unwin.

Foster, L. and Stockley, D. (1988) *Australian Multiculturalism: A Documentary History and Critique*. Clevedon, Avon: Multilingual Matters Ltd.

Fowler, R. (1983) Sexually inclusive curriculum, *Victorian Secondary Teacher*, September: 12–17.

Goodall, H., Jakubowicz, A., Martin, J. *et al.* (1991) *Racism, Cultural Pluralism and the Media: A Report to the Office of Multicultural Affairs*. Sydney School of Humanities Faculty of Social Science, Sydney: University of Technology.

Gore, J. (1992) What we can do for you! What can 'we' do for 'you'? Struggling over empowerment in critical and feminist pedagogy, in C. Luke and J. Gore (eds) *Feminisms and Critical Pedagogy*. New York: Routledge.

Gunew, S. (1994) *Framing Marginality: Multicultural Literary Studies*. Carlton, Vic.: Melbourne University Press.

Gunew, S. and Longley, K. (eds) (1992) *Striking Chords: Multicultural Literary Interpretation*. Sydney: Allen & Unwin.

Gunew, S. and Rizvi, F. (eds) (1994) *Culture, Difference and the Arts*. St Leonards, NSW: Allen & Unwin.

Gunew, S. and Yeatman, A. (eds) (1993) *Feminism and the Politics of Difference*. St Leonards, NSW: Allen & Unwin.

Hage, G. (1998) *White Nation: Fantasies of White Supremacy in a Multicultural Society*. Sydney: Pluto Press/Comerford and Miller.

Hall, S. (1996a) What is this 'black' in black popular culture?, in D. Morely and K. Chen (eds) *Stuart Hall: Critical Dialogues in Cultural Studies*. New York and London: Routledge.

Hall, S. (1996b) The meaning of new times, in D. Morely, and K. Chen (eds) *Stuart Hall: Critical Dialogues in Cultural Studies*. New York and London: Routledge.

Hamilton, A. (1975) Aboriginal women: the means of production, in J. Mercer (ed.) *The Other Half: Women in Australian Society*. Ringwood, Victoria: Pelican.

Haw, K. (1998) *Educating Muslim Girls: Shifting Discourses*. Buckingham: Open University Press.

hooks, b., (1981) *Ain't I a Woman: Black Women and Feminism*. London: Pluto Press.

hooks, b., (1984) *Feminist Theory: From Margin to Center*. Boston, MA: South End Press.

hooks, b., (1989) *Talking Back: Thinking Feminist, Thinking Black*. London: Sheeba Feminist Publishers and Boston, MA: South End Press.

hooks, b., (1990) *Yearning: Race, Gender, and Cultural Politics*. Boston, MA: South End Press.

hooks, b. (1992) *Black Looks: Race and Representation*. Boston, MA: South End Press.

Huggins, J. (1991) Black women and women's liberation, in S. Gunew (ed.) *A Reader in Feminist Knowledge*. London: Routledge.

Huggins, J. and Saunders, K. (1993) Defying the ethnographic ventriloquists: race, gender and the legacies of colonialism, *Lilith: A Feminist History Journal*, 8: 60–70.

Hughes, R. (1988) *The Fatal Shore*. London: Pan.

Human Rights and Equal Opportunity Commission (1991) *Report of the National Inquiry into Racist Violence*. Canberra: Australian Government Publishing Service.

Inglis, C. (1993) Turkish-Australian youth and educational change, *Migration Action*, 15(2): 19–21.

Inglis, C., Elley, J. and Manderson, L. (1992) *Making Something of Myself: Educational Attainment and Social and Economic Mobility of Turkish Australian Young People*. Canberra: AGPS for the Office of Multicultural Affairs.

Interim Committee for the Australian Schools Commission (1973) *Schools in Australia: Report of the Interim Committee for the Australian Schools Commission*. Canberra: AGPS.

Jakubowicz, A. (1981) State and ethnicity: multiculturalism as ideology, *Australian and New Zealand Journal of Sociology*, 17(3): 4–13.

Jakubowicz, A. and Castles, S. (1986) The inherent subjectivity of the apparently objective in research on ethnicity and class. Paper presented at Sociology Association of Australia and New Zealand Conference, July.

Jakubowicz, A., Morrissy, M. and Palser, J. (1984) *Ethnicity, Class and Social Policy in Australia*. Kensington, NSW: Social Welfare Research Centre, University of New South Wales.

Kalantzis, M. (1987) Aspirations, participation and outcomes: from research to a curriculum project for reform, in V. Foster (ed.) *Including Girls: Curriculum Perspectives on the Education of Girls*. Canberra: Work Opportunities for Women Project, Curriculum Development Centre.

Kalantzis, M. and Cope, B. (1984) Multiculturalism and education policy, in G. Bottomley and M. de Lepervanche (eds) *Ethnicity, Class and Gender in Australia*. Sydney: Allen & Unwin.

Kalantzis, M. and Cope, B. (1987) Cultural differences, gender differences: social literacy and inclusive curriculum, *Curriculum Perspectives*, 7(1): 64–8.

Kamboureli, S. (ed.) (1996) *Making a Difference: Canadian Multicultural Literature*. Don Mills, Ontario: Oxford University Press.

Kasem, A.-H. (1988) *Report on the Educational Needs and Interests of Disadvantaged Arabic Speaking Youth*. Melbourne: Council of Adult Education.

Kenway, J. and Willis, S. with Blackmore, J. and Rennie, L. (1997) *Answering Back: Girls, Boys and Feminism in Schools*. St Leonards, NSW: Allen & Unwin.

Kisrwani, J. (1989) HELP: what is going on (part II), *Al-Minbar*, October: 13.

Klug, F. (1989) 'Oh to be in England': the British case study, in N. Yuval-Davis and F. Anthias (eds) *Woman–Nation–State*. London: Macmillan.

Kunek, S. (1993) *The Brides*. Kew, Victoria: Kunexion.

Laclau, E. and Mouffe, C. (1985) *Hegemony and Socialist Strategy: Towards a Radical Democratic Politics*. London and New York: Verso.

Lawrence, E. (1982a) In the abundance of water the fool is thirsty: sociology and black 'Pathology', in Centre for Contemporary Cultural Studies (eds) *The Empire Strikes Back*. London: Hutchinson.

Lawrence, E. (1982b) Just plain common sense: the 'roots of racism', in Centre for Contemporary Cultural Studies (eds) *The Empire Strikes Back*. London: Hutchinson.

Lever-Tracy, C. (1984) A new Australian working class leadership: the case of Ford Broadmeadows, in G. Bottomley and M. de Lepervanche (eds) *Ethnicity, Class and Gender in Australia*. Sydney: Allen & Unwin.

Lewis, M. (1993) *Without a Word: Teaching Beyond Women's Silence*. New York and London: Routledge.

Lingard, B. and Douglas, P. (1999) *Men Engaging Feminisms: Pro-feminism, Backlashes and Schooling*. Buckingham: Open University Press.

Lo Bianco, J. (1986) in Foreword, G. Tsolidis, *Educating Voula: A Report on Non-English Speaking Background Girls and Education*. Melbourne: Ministry of Education of Victoria.

Loh, M. (1980) *With Courage in their Cases*. Melbourne: Italian Federation of Emigrant Workers.

London, H. I. (1970) *Non-White Immigration and the 'White Australia' Policy*. New York: New York University Press.

Lorde, A. (1984) The master's tools can never dismantle the master's house, in *Sister Outsider*. Freedom, CA: The Crossing Press.

McCarthy, C. and Crichlow, W. (eds) (1990) *Race and Curriculum: Social Inequality and the Theories and Politics of Difference in Contemporary Research on Schooling*. London and Philadelphia, PA: Falmer Press.

McConville, C. (1987) *Croppies, Celts and Catholics: The Irish in Australia*. Caulfield East, Victoria: Edward Arnold.

Macintyre, S. (1985) *Winners and Losers*. Sydney: Allen & Unwin.

MACMME (Ministerial Advisory Committee on Multicultural and Migrant Education) (1984) *Ministerial Advisory Committee on Multicultural and Migrant Education 1983/84 Annual Report*. Ministry of Education, Victoria.

MACMME (undated) *In Our Own Words*. Students' book and teachers' handbook. Melbourne: Ministry of Education of Victoria.

MACMME (1986) *Helping Your Daughter Attain her Aspirations*. Pamphlet produced in 14 community languages. Melbourne: Ministry of Education of Victoria.

MACMME (1987) *Switch It On Miss*. Melbourne: Ministry of Education of Victoria.

MACMME (1988) *Mother Tongue*. Video and study notes. Melbourne: Ministry of Education of Victoria.

McQueen, H. (1986) *A New Britannia: An Argument Concerning the Social Origins of Australian Radicalism and Nationalism*. Ringwood, Vic.: Penguin.

Mama, A. (1984) Black women, the economic crisis and the British state, *Feminist Review*, 17: 21–35.

Marjoribanks, K. (1978) Ethnicity, family environment, school attitudes and academic achievement, *Australian Journal of Education*, 22(3). Reprinted in P. De Lacey and M. Poole (eds) (1979) *Mosaic or Melting Pot*. Sydney: Harcourt Brace Jovanovich.

Marjoribanks, K. (1980) *Ethnic Families and Children's Achievements*. Sydney: Allen & Unwin.

Martin, J. (1983) The development of multiculturalism, in Committee of Review of the Australian Institute of Multicultural Affairs, *Report to the Minister for Immigration and Ethnic Affairs, Volume II*, November 1983. Canberra: AGPS.

Martin, J. (1984) Non English-speaking women: production and reproduction, in G. Bottomley and M. de Lepervanche (eds) *Ethnicity, Class and Gender in Australia.* Sydney: Allen & Unwin.

Martin, J. (1996) Non-English-speaking migrant women in Australia, in E. Vasta and S. Castles (eds) *The Teeth are Smiling: The Persistence of Racism in Multicultural Australia.* St Leonards, NSW: Allen & Unwin.

Martin, J. and Meade, P. (1979) *The Educational Experience of Sydney High School Students: A Comparative Study of Migrant Students of Non English Speaking Origin and Students Who Were Born in an English Speaking Country.* Canberra: Department of Education.

Mathews, J. M. (1997) Racism and the construction of 'Asian' femininity, in J. Gill and M. Dyer (eds) *School Days: Past, Present and Future. Education of Girls in Twentieth Century Australia.* Magill, South Australia: Research Centre for Gender Studies in SA.

Miles, R. (1988) Beyond the 'race' concept: the reproduction of racism in England, in M. de Lepervanche and G. Bottomley (eds) *The Cultural Construction of Race.* Sydney Studies in Society and Culture 4. Sydney: University of Sydney.

Miller, P.W. (1984) Teenage unemployment: the role of education and migration, in R. Castle and J. Mangan (eds) *Unemployment in the Eighties.* Melbourne: Longman Cheshire.

Miller, P.W. and Volker, P. (1987) *The Youth Labour Market in Australia: A Survey of the Issues and Evidence.* Canberra: Centre for Economic Policy Research, Australian National University.

Minister of Education (1985) *Ministerial Papers 1–6.* Victoria: Minister of Education.

Mohanty, C. (1991) Under western eyes: feminist scholarship and colonial discourses, in C. Mohanty, A. Russo, and L. Torres (eds) *Third World Women and the Politics of Feminism.* Bloomington, IN: Indiana University Press.

Myhill, M., Herriman, M. and Mulligan, D. (1994) *Subject and Career Choice of NESB Youth.* Canberra: AGPS.

Ng, I. (1995) 'I'm a feminist but . . .'. Other women and postnational feminism, in B. Caine and R. Pringle (eds) *Transitions: New Australian Feminisms.* St Leonards, NSW: Allen & Unwin.

Nicholson, L. J. (ed.) (1990) *Feminism/Postmodernism.* New York: Routledge.

Office of the Minister of Ethnic Affairs (undated) *Ministerial Discussion Paper: Racism in the 1980's* [sic]: *A Response.* Victoria: Office of the Minister of Ethnic Affairs.

Pallotta-Chiarolli, M. (1999) *Tapestry.* Milsons Point, NSW: Random House.

Pankhurst, F. (1984) *Research Report: Workplace Child Care and Migrant Parents, National Women's Advisory Council.* Canberra: AGPS.

Parmar, P. (1982) Gender, race and class: Asian women in resistance, in Centre for Contemporary Cultural Studies (eds) *The Empire Strikes Back.* London: Hutchinson.

Pettman, J. (1992) *Living in the Margins: Racism, Sexism and Feminism in Australia.* Sydney: Allen & Unwin.

Phoenix, A. (1990) Theories of gender and black families, in T. Lovell (ed.) *British Feminist Thought*. Oxford: Basil Blackwell.

Price, C. A. (1963) *Southern Europeans in Australia*. Melbourne: Oxford University Press.

Ramazanoglu, C. (1989) *Feminism and the Contradictions of Oppression*. London: Routledge.

Reynolds, H. (1996) *Aboriginal Sovereignty: Reflections on Race, State and Nation*. St Leonards, NSW: Allen & Unwin.

Rizvi, F. (1996) Racism, reorientation and the cultural politics of Asia–Australia relations, in E. Vasta and S. Castles (eds) *The Teeth are Smiling: The Persistence of Racism in Multicultural Australia*. St Leonards, NSW: Allen & Unwin.

Sadaawi, N. El (1980) Arab women and western feminism: an interview with Nawal El Sadaawi, *Race and Class*, 22(2): 175–82.

Schools Commission (1975a) *Girls, School and Society: Report by a Study Group to the Schools Commission*. Canberra: Schools Commission.

Schools Commission (1975b) *Report for the Triennium 1976–1978*. Canberra: Australian Government Publishing Service.

Scott, J.W. (1990) Deconstructing equality-versus-difference: or, the uses of post-structuralist theory for feminism' in M. Hirsch and E. Fox Keller (eds) *Conflicts in Feminism*. New York: Routledge.

Secretariat to the Committee to Advise on Australia's Immigration Policies (1987) *Understanding Immigration*. Canberra: Australian Government Publishing Service.

Sheldrake, P. (1985) A study of migrant unemployment, in Federation of Ethnic Communities' Councils of Australia (FECCA), First National Congress, Sixth National Conference and AGM (Proceedings), Melbourne, December 1984. Melbourne: FECCA.

Smith, V. (1990) Split affinities: the case of interracial rape, in M. Hirsch and E. Fox Keller (eds) *Conflicts in Feminism*. New York: Routledge.

Spivak, G. C. (1990) *The Post-Colonial Critic*. New York: Routledge.

Spivak, G. C. (1993) *Outside in the Teaching Machine*. New York and London: Routledge.

Storer, D. (undated) '*But I Wouldn't Want my Wife to Work Here . . .*'. Melbourne: Centre for Urban Research and Action.

Strinzos, M. (1984) To be Greek is to be good, in L. Johnson and D. Tyler (eds) *Cultural Politics*. Melbourne Working Papers Series 5. Melbourne: Sociology Research Group in Cultural and Educational Studies, Melbourne University.

Summers, A. (1975) *Damned Whores and God's Police: The Colonization of Women in Australia*. Blackburn, Vic.: Penguin.

Suzuki, D. and Oiwa, K. (1996) *The Japan We Never Knew: A Journey of Discovery*. Toronto: Stoddart.

Sykes, B. (1975) Black women in Australia: a history, in J. Mercer (ed.) *The Other Half: Women in Australian Society*. Ringwood, Vic.: Penguin.

Taft, R. (1975) *The Career Aspirations of Immigrant School Children in Victoria*. La Trobe Sociology Papers 12. Bundoora, Vic.: Department of Sociology, La Trobe University.

Teese, R., McLean, G. and Polesel, J. (1993) *Equity Outcomes: A Report to the Schools Council's Task Force on a Broadbanded Equity Program for Schools*. Canberra: National Board of Employment, Education and Training.

Thomas, C. (1980) Girls and counter-school culture, in D. MacCallum and U. Ozolins (eds) *Melbourne Working Papers*. Melbourne: Education Department, Melbourne University.

Tsolidis, G. (1986) *Educating Voula: A Report on Non-English Speaking Background Girls and Education*. Melbourne: Ministry of Education of Victoria.

Tsolidis, G. (series ed.) (1989) *Ethnic Minority Women Sharing their Experiences*, series of seven books under various titles. Canberra: Curriculum Development Centre.

Tsolidis, G. (1990) Ethnic minority girls and self-esteem, in J. Kenway and S. Willis (eds) *Hearts and Minds: Self-Esteem and the Schooling of Girls*. London: Falmer Press.

Tsolidis, G. (1993a) Difference and identity: a feminist debate indicating directions for the development of a transformative curriculum, in L. Yates (ed.) *Feminism and Education: Melbourne Studies in Education*. Bundoora, Victoria: La Trobe University Press.

Tsolidis, G. (1993b) Re-envisioning multiculturalism within a feminist framework, *Journal of Intercultural Studies*, 14(2): 1–12.

Tsolidis, G. (1995a) Greek-Australian families, in R. Hartley (ed.) *Families and Cultural Diversity*. St Leonards, NSW: Allen & Unwin and Australian Institute of Family Studies.

Tsolidis, G. (1995b) Progressive purposes and large data-bases: constructions, critiques and contexts, Australian Association for Research in Education, Hobart, November.

Tsolidis, G. (1996a) Feminist theorisations of identity and difference: a case-study related to gender education policy, *British Journal of Sociology of Education*, 17(3): 267–77.

Tsolidis, G. (1996b) Where have all the banners gone? Teaching to a feminist politics within the academy, *Discourse: Studies in the Cultural Politics of Education*, 17(2): 271–7.

Tsolidis, G. (1999) Diasporic maternity: Australia, Canada and Greece. Paper presented at the Nationalism Identity Minority Rights: Sociological and Political Perspectives Conference, Bristol University, 16–19 September.

Vasta, E. and Castles, S. (eds) (1996) *The Teeth are Smiling: The Persistence of Racism in Multicultural Australia*, St Leonards, NSW: Allen & Unwin.

Victorian Committee on Equal Opportunity in Schools (1977) *Victorian Committee on Equal Opportunity in Schools: Report to the Premier of Victoria, July 1977*. Melbourne: Government Printer.

Victorian Committee to Advise the Attorney-General on Racial Vilification (1992) *Racial Vilification in Victoria: Report of the Committee to Advise the Attorney-General on Racial Vilification*. Melbourne: Victorian Committee to Advise the Attorney-General on Racial Vilification.

White, R. (1985) *Inventing Australia: Images and Identity 1688–1980*. Sydney: Allen & Unwin.

Women's Bureau, Department of Employment and Youth Affairs (1981) *The Role of Women in the Economy*. Canberra: AGPS.

Yates, L. (1985) Is 'girls-friendly' schooling really what girls need? Some reflections on the Australian experience, in J. Whyte, R. Deem, L. Kant and M. Cruikshank (eds) *Girl Friendly Schooling*. London: Methuen.

Yates, L. (1987a) Inclusive curriculum, *Curriculum Perspectives*, 7(1): 57–8.

Yates, L. (1987b) Curriculum theory and non-sexist education: A discussion of curriculum theory, feminist theory and Victorian education policy and practice 1975–1985. PhD thesis, La Trobe University, Bundoora, Vic.

Yates, L. (1988) Does 'all' students include girls? A discussion of recent policy, practice and theory, *Australian Educational Researcher*, 15(1): 41–57.

Yates, L. (ed.) (1993a) *Feminism and Education*. Melbourne Studies in Education. Bundoora, Vic.: La Trobe University Press.

Yates, L. (1993b) *The Education of Girls: Policy, Research and the Question of Gender*. Hawthorn: Australian Council for Educational Research.

Yates, L. (1998) Dreams of the future in an era of change: longitudinal qualitative research speaks back to policy studies. Paper presented at the American Educational Research Association conference, San Diego, CA, April.

Yates, L. and Leder, G. (1996) *Student Pathways: A Review and Overview of National Databases on Gender Equity*. Tuggeranong, Australian Capital Territory: Department of Education and Training and Children's, Youth and Family Bureau.

Yeatman, A. (1991) Postmodern epistemological politics and social science. Paper presented at the Third Annual Conference of the Australian Sociology Association, Brisbane, 30 November–2 December.

Yeatman, A. (1994) *Postmodern Revisionings of the Political*. New York: Routledge.

York, B. (1990) *Empire and Race: The Maltese in Australia 1881–1949*. Kensington, NSW: University Press.

Young, I. (1990) The ideal of community and the politics of difference, in L. Nicholson (ed.) *Feminism/Postmodernism*. New York and London: Routledge.

Young, I. (1997) *Intersecting Voices: Dilemmas of Gender, Political Philosophy and Policy*. Princeton, NJ: Princeton University Press.

Yuval-Davis N. (1986) Ethnic/racial divisions and the nation in Britain and Australia, *Capital and Class*, 28: 87–103.

Yuval-Davis, N. (1997) *Gender and Nation*. London: Sage.

Yuval-Davis, N. and Anthias, F. (eds) (1989) *Woman–Nation–State*. London: Macmillan Press.

Yuval-Davis, N. and Werbner, P. (eds) (1999) *Women, Citizenship and Difference*. London: Zed.

# Index